THE RISE
OF CHRISTIAN
EUROPE

THE RISE
OF CHRISTIAN
EUROPE

HUGH TREVOR-ROPER

with 124 illustrations, 17 in color

 W. W. NORTON & COMPANY

ISBN 0-393-95802-7

W. W. Norton & Company, Inc., 500 Fifth Avenue, New York, N Y 10110
W. W. Norton & Company, Ltd., 37 Great Russell Street, London WC1B 3NU

Printed in Singapore

1 2 3 4 5 6 7 8 9 0

CONTENTS

MAPS

FOREWORD

The substance of this book was originally delivered as a series of lectures to the University of Sussex in October 1963, and relayed by BBC Television. As delivered, they were printed in *The Listener* in November and December 1963. Since delivering them, I have revised them for publication, correcting some small errors of fact which have been pointed out to me and expanding some passages which the limitation of time had originally forced me to compress. I hope that the former process has left them less vulnerable to those professional medievalists who, I read, are 'sharpening their knives' against me, and that the latter has made them clearer to my less erudite readers who, I hope, will be more indulgent.

Not that I expect, by any change that I can make, to escape the criticism of the experts. Doubtless, in these lectures, I have walked unwarily into hornets' nests of controversy and shown a deplorable unfamiliarity with certain profound theses. Nevertheless I am prepared to take the risk. Historians, I believe, should study the process of history and not merely the detail of the narrow sector in which, perforce, they specialize; and if this means that they must occasionally trespass into less familiar sectors, they must be prepared for the consequences. They know that, as they swish through that long series of jealously tended and strongly fenced small-holdings, many a barbed prickle, and perhaps a few peppery pellets, will be embedded in their happily thickened skin. However, all in all, the pleasure (I find) outweighs the danger. So also, perhaps, does the profit. It is pleasant, and it is profitable for a historian to turn occasionally to fresh and less familiar fields, and there to apply the techniques and test the theories which he has developed in his own narrower studies. If I have applied them usefully—if this attempt, by a modern historian, to look synoptically at the Middle Ages, succeeds in stimulating questions about history in general—I shall hope to be forgiven for the incidental errors which, no doubt, I have committed, and I shall contrive not to flinch too abjectly at the sight of those gleaming, sharpened, medieval knives.

HUGH TREVOR-ROPER

Chiefswood,
Melrose,
Scotland
8 August 1964

I THE STAGES OF PROGRESS

It is fashionable to speak today as if European history were devalued: as if historians, in the past, have paid too much attention to it; and as if, nowadays, we should pay less. Undergraduates, seduced, as always, by the changing breath of journalistic fashion, demand that they should be taught the history of black Africa. Perhaps, in the future, there will be some African history to teach. But at present there is none, or very little: there is only the history of the Europeans in Africa. The rest is largely darkness, like the history of pre-European, pre-Columbian America. And darkness is not a subject for history.

Please do not misunderstand me. I do not deny that men existed even in dark countries and dark centuries, nor that they had political life and culture, interesting to sociologists and anthropologists; but history, I believe, is essentially a form of movement, and purposive movement too. It is not a mere phantasmagoria of changing shapes and costumes, of battles and conquests, dynasties and usurpations, social forms and social disintegration. If all history is equal, as some now believe, there is no reason why we should study one section of it rather than another; for certainly we cannot study it all. Then indeed we may neglect our own history and amuse ourselves with the unrewarding gyrations of barbarous tribes in picturesque but irrelevant corners of the globe: tribes whose chief function in history, in my opinion, is to show to the present an image of the past from which, by history, it has escaped; or shall I seek to avoid the indignation of the medievalists by saying, from which it has changed?

For on this subject, I believe, with the great historians of the eighteenth century, whom I find very good company (the good sense of the ancients is often more illuminating than the documented pedantry of the moderns), that history, or rather the study of history, has a purpose. We study it not merely for amusement—though it can be amusing—but in order to discover how we have come to where we are. In the eighteenth century men certainly studied Afro-Asian *society*. Turn over the pages of the great French and Scottish writers—Montesquieu, Voltaire, Hume, Adam Smith, Millar. Their interest in non-European society is obvious. Indeed, in order to found the new science of sociology—one of the great intellectual contributions of the Enlightenment—they turned deliberately away from Europe. They read the accounts of European missionaries and drew general deductions from the customs of Otaheite and the Caribbees. But with Afro-Asian history, as distinct from society, they had little patience. When Dr Johnson bestowed excessive praise on a certain old *History of the Turks*, Gibbon pulled him up sharply: 'An enlightened age', he replied, would not be satisfied with '1,300 folio pages of speeches and battles': it 'requires from the historian some tincture of philosophy and criticism'. 'If all you have to tell us', said Voltaire, in his advice to contemporary historians, 'is that one barbarian succeeded another barbarian on the banks of the Oxus or the Jaxartes, what benefit have you conferred on the public?' And David Hume, pushing his way briskly through 'the obscure and uninteresting period of the Saxon annals', remarked that it was 'fortunate for letters' that so much of the barbarous detail was 'buried in silence and oblivion'. 'What instruction or entertainment can it give the reader' he asked 'to hear a long bead-roll of barbarous names, Egric, Annas, Ethelbert, Ethelwald, Aldulf, Elfwold, Beorne, Ethelred, Ethelbert, who successively murdered, expelled, or inherited from each other, and obscurely filled the throne' of East Anglia? This is not to say that Hume was indifferent to problems of Anglo-Saxon society. His brilliant appendix on that subject disproves any such suggestion. But he distinguished between society and history. To him, as to all these writers, whig or tory, radical or conservative, the positive content of history consisted not in the meaningless fermentation of passive or barbarous societies but in the movement of society, the process, conscious or unconscious, by which certain societies, at certain times, had risen out of the barbarism once common to all, and, by their efforts and example, by the interchange and diffusion of arts and sciences, gradually drawn or driven other societies along with them to 'the full light and freedom of the eighteenth century'.

Today, though it is fashionable to be more sceptical about the light and freedom, I do not think that the essential function of history has changed. And if the function has not changed, the substance has not changed either. It may well be that the future will be the future of non-European peoples: that the 'colonial' peoples of Africa and Asia will inherit that primacy in the world which the 'imperialist' West can no longer sustain. Such shifts in the centre of political gravity in the world, such replacement of imperialist powers by their former colonies, have often happened in the past. Mediterranean Europe was once, in the Dark Ages, a colony of Islam; and northern Europe was afterwards, in the Middle Ages, a colony of the Mediterranean. But even if that should happen, it would not alter the past. The new rulers of the world, whoever they may be, will inherit a position that has been built up by Europe, and by Europe alone. It is European techniques, European examples, European ideas which have shaken the non-European world out of its past—out of barbarism in Africa, out of a far older, slower, more majestic civilization in Asia; and the history of the world, for the last five centuries, in so far as it has significance, has been European history. I do not think we need make any apology if our study of history is Europa-centric.

I have said 'for the last five centuries': that is, roughly from the time of the Italian Renaissance and the great European discoveries. Of course great movements such as this cannot be exactly dated. History is an untidy process which does not fit into the exact compartments in which, perforce, we study it. The present, which contains the seeds of the future, is always heavily loaded with the past, and a general movement may begin here and there at different times. Still, making all these allowances, we may take the later fifteenth century as the beginning of the European 'break-through', the time from which the equal or oscillating balance of civilization in the world was gradually but emphatically overturned.

Consider for a moment that old balance, the balance as it stood before this 'break-through'. In the fifteenth century there were many civilized societies in the world, and there was no particular reason to suppose that any one of them was destined to overshadow, or conquer, or absorb the others. The great Arab historian, Ibn Khaldoun, the profoundest, most exciting historical writer between Antiquity and the Renaissance, who wrote his monumental work of philosophy and history in the late fourteenth century in a castle in Algeria, surrounded by desolation and barbarians, listed these societies in order, all along the temperate zone, from the Franks of Europe to China of the Ming. All had their separate cultures, their different qualities, but there was no hint then that it was the 'Franks' who held the secret of the future. It is true, the Italian merchants, whom Ibn Khaldoun saw in the ports of North Africa, astonished him by their wealth, while the Arab world around him—at least the Arab world in North Africa—seemed, by some social mechanism which he sought to explain, to be in decline. But the Mediterranean was not the whole world, nor was southern Europe only to be compared with North Africa. There was Persia, there was India, there was

1 The China which impressed Marco Polo. The Master of the Mint puts the official seal on paper money in the presence of the Great Khan

China. A century earlier, the Italian merchants who had found their way to Mongol China had felt very small among the magnificence of Chinese society. Marco Polo, when he returned to Venice, had been known as Messer Millioni because, like some dazzled novice in a millionaire's mansion, he could not stop talking about the millions; and the China of the Ming was certainly no less magnificent than the China of the Mongols. Even three centuries after Marco Polo, the Italian Giovanni Botero, the theorist of the splendid princes of the European Counter-Reformation, would insist that even the greatest cities of sixteenth-century Europe—and he was an expert and wrote a study of them—were poor things compared with the cities of China, as they had been described to him by the Jesuit missionaries and European merchants whom he used to buttonhole on the quay at Genoa.

Moreover, in the time of Ibn Khaldoun in the late fourteenth century, it was not only Islam—the old Islam of Iraq and Syria and Egypt and north-west Africa—that seemed to be in decline. Christen-

2 Map of the world, used by the fourteenth-century Arab historian Ibn Khaldoun in his *Muqaddimah*, or 'Introduction to History'. The cartographer's view of the world is inverted: the Mediterranean countries and the Near East are in the lower right-hand quarter, disproportionately large. China is in the lower left. The large area south of the equator (i.e. above the top latitudinal line) is 'empty because of the heat'. The whole earth is ringed by a 'surrounding sea'

3 The decline of the Middle Ages: this *danse macabre*, from a French wall-painting of *c.* 146

dom, for all its new prosperity, seemed then to be sinking too. We tend to forget this. We look—how can we avoid looking?—at the past from the present, and we see the fifteenth century as the century of the Renaissance, of the great discoveries, the beginning of a long process of expansion. But it is only in historical perspective that it appears thus: perhaps only in modern perspective too. It was not till the eighteenth century that men looked back and saw the period of the Renaissance—or rather, as they called it, the 'Revival of Letters' —as the beginning of a new age, a revolution, as Voltaire wrote, which changed everything, 'as has happened again in our own time'. It was not till the mid-nineteenth century that the term 'Renaissance' was coined. It was coined, I understand, by the French historian Jules Michelet in 1840; it was established by Jacob Burckhardt with his book *The Civilization of the Renaissance* in 1860. But to the Europeans of the fifteenth and even of the early sixteenth centuries, it did not seem that they were on the threshold of a new age of expansion. The fifteenth century has been described by the Dutch historian Huizinga as 'the waning of the Middle Ages'. To the Europeans of the Middle Ages, who knew no other, who did not

ifies the introversion and gloom of Christendom, on the eve of the great discoveries

know that they were in the 'Middle Ages'—the term only came gradually into use, in the seventeenth century, as the reality receded.

This sense of general decline in Christendom is obvious if we listen to the voice of the time. Again and again we hear it. Now that the world is drawing to its end, men say—it is a kind of refrain—we must do something about it. What must we do? We must eat, drink, and be merry, say some, and they enjoy the Renaissance. We must repent of our sins and reform our ways, say others, and they bring in the Reformation. I over-simplify, of course, but my point remains. The years before the Reformation did not necessarily seem to contemporaries a period of excitement, of promise, of hope. In some ways they may have seemed so, and to some men; but in other ways, and to other men, they seemed, and might reasonably seem, years of depression and decline. That depressed mood is preserved for us in the monuments of the time, with their *triumphs of death*, their *danses macabres*—those varying figures of kings, bishops, knights, merchants, craftsmen, etc., all dancing with the unvarying figure of death—and their monumental *memento mori*: that severe

4 The *memento mori*. The image of putrefaction lurks beneath the serene, ageless monumental effigy (*c.* 1475) of Alice, Duchess of Suffolk in the parish church of Ewelme, Oxon

lesson in stone which we can find in so many of our own parish churches. Above, serene and recumbent, lies the funeral effigy, fresh with a stylized freshness (for it is always represented at the age of thirty, the age of Christ's resurrection). Below, behind a grille, we discover reality in the grim, grinning image of putrefaction.

Those who believed, in the later fifteenth and early sixteenth centuries, that Christian civilization was declining around them had not far to look for the evidence. Did they believe in liberty? When they looked about them, they saw the free cities of Europe, the manufactories of medieval culture, folding up: their lights going out, one by one. Did they believe in Christendom? But the area of Christendom itself was shrinking as the Turks crept irresistibly forward, swallowing up Christendom and old Islam alike: first the Balkans, then Constantinople itself, then Albania, then Egypt;

finally, in successive years, Belgrade and Rhodes, the land and sea bastions of the West. Meanwhile Italy itself, the spiritual and economic capital of the West, the source alike of religious authority and municipal freedom, of eastern trade and western culture, was dissolving in anarchy and conquest. It had been invaded, partitioned, subjected: and the subjection would last for three centuries. Italy, said a sixteenth-century pope, used to be a well-tuned instrument of four harmonious strings—Milan, Venice, Rome, and Naples; now the instrument was broken and the strings were jarred and discordant in barbarian hands.

In the face of such losses, of what value, men asked, was the new 'expansion of Europe': the crossing of the Atlantic, the rounding of the Cape of Good Hope, the 'discovery' of the East—events which seem to us, in retrospect, so tremendous a forward step? Just as Voltaire, in the eighteenth century, dismissed Canada, for which the French and British were fighting in the Seven Years' War, as 'quelques arpents de neige'—a few acres of snow; just as Disraeli, on the eve of the nineteenth-century imperialism of which he himself was to become the prophet, dismissed 'those wretched colonies' as 'millstones round our necks'; so the men of the fifteenth and early sixteenth centuries thought little of their oceanic gains compared with their continental losses. 'We set out to conquer worthless new empires beyond the seas', lamented Busbequius, the highly intelligent Belgian whom the King of the Romans sent as ambassador to the Sultan of Turkey, 'and we are losing the heart of Europe.' Christendom, he wrote, subsisted precariously by the good will of the Sophy —the King of Persia whose ambitions in the East continually called the Sultan of Turkey back from his western conquests. Columbus, it is well known, had great difficulty in finding backers for his famous voyage, nor did the kings of Spain, to whom he gave a new world, pay much attention to his gift. Having hoped for a new route to the populous, golden East, they were disappointed with savage islands and a waste continent. Like most new colonies—like New England in the seventeenth and Australia in the eighteenth century —America was seen, at first, largely as a vent for waste population, not a source of strength.

Admittedly there is another side to the picture. Humanity is too complex to confine itself within one mood. The men who actually sent out, or financed, or made the great voyages were inspired by a more dynamic faith. We catch the echo of it in *The Lusiads*, the epic poem in which the Portuguese poet Camoēs celebrated the voyage of Vasco da Gama to India round the Cape. Camoēs breathes the confidence and exhilaration of one who has gazed on new horizons: he describes men who have tasted the forbidden fruit and will displace the gods from their thrones. On the other hand we should remember that Camoēs wrote seventy years after the event, when the new age really had begun. Immediately after the first great discoveries, the discoveries associated with Prince Henry the Navigator, there had been a reaction in Portugal against these unprofitable oceanic follies, and the Portuguese ruling class returned

5 Preliminary sheet, with privilege and licence, of the first edition of Luis de Camoes' epic of discovery *The Lusiads*, published at Lisbon in 1571

for a time to the more traditional exercise of raiding their neighbours' backyards. Only later, when the perilous new voyages had begun to bring in a regular profit, did a new generation of Portuguese noblemen think it time to invest in the new Empire, following the example of their own monarch, whom his envious royal neighbours snobbishly described as 'the Grocer King'.

For no generation of human history has one character only. History is not as simple as that. Always there are tensions: tensions of class, tensions of generations, tensions of mood. The sixteenth century may be, in many ways, a century of expansion; but it also has its under-current of gloom. The Emperor Charles V, for whom, as King of Spain, Cortés was conquering Mexico and Pizarro Peru, kept his eyes grimly fixed on Europe, wearing himself out in ceaseless, joyless struggle to maintain a crumbling edifice: a struggle

6, 7 Titian's portrait shows the pensive, pessimistic Charles V, whose European empire was in danger even while the ships of Cortés were successfully attacking Xolloco (1519) during their conquest of Mexico (*right*)

8 Michelangelo's figure of
Lorenzo de' Medici, seated
on his tomb in the Medici
Chapel in Florence, expresses
the brooding melancholy of
sixteenth-century Italy

which he only suspended to play with his clocks or his organ and to
anticipate, with gloomy relish, his own funeral. 'The profound sad-
ness of that time', says a great art historian, 'has been expressed by
Michelangelo in the tombs of the Medici: his figures seem to have
given up all hope and to look on life with disdain or to sink into
sleep. Pope Clement VII thought that the prophecies of the Apoca-
lypse were about to be fulfilled, and that the end of the world was
at hand; and so, before dying, he ordered Michelangelo to paint on
the wall of the Sistine Chapel the *Last Judgment*.'

Yet this Europe, or rather, as men then said, this Christendom (for Christendom, which had once embraced Africa and hither Asia, was now confined to Europe, shrunk to its smallest extent, perhaps, since the end of the Roman Empire)—this Christendom, which seemed so devitalized, so attenuated, so corrupted, so fragile, had in itself the springs of a new and enormous vitality. It was from the time of the Renaissance, from the years around 1500, that the 'philosophers' of the eighteenth century, the first Christian thinkers to see history as a process—or at least as a social, not a theological, process—dated the continuous rise of Europe to the domination of the world. In the nineteenth century, when Marx gave an economic interpretation of that phenomenal rise, it was in the same period, in the sixteenth century, that he discovered the beginnings of that 'capitalism' which, he believed, had been the motor of conquest. And in the twentieth century, when Werner Sombart and Max Weber looked for the spiritual origins of the effort which realized itself in capitalism, it was once again in that period, the period of the Reformation, that they found it—whether they found it (like Sombart) in the dispersal of the Peninsular Jews or (like Weber) in the new doctrines of the Reformation.

Today few of these explanations are accepted. We do not believe that capitalism began in the sixteenth century, nor that it was created by Jews, nor even by Protestants; at least not as simply as that. But we still believe that the age of the Renaissance was the beginning of an almost continuous process of European advance; and therefore we are still faced by a problem, which is perhaps a more difficult problem because these relatively simple solutions no longer convince us. The problem is: how had Europe acquired this position? How had the 'barbarian', 'feudal', 'gothic' kingdoms of the West, whose whole structure and character and way of life and values would seem to us today, if we were to look at it with eyes unconditioned by explanation and interpretation, so primitive, savage, and bizarre—how had they acquired this internal dynamism which was to carry them forward not merely to the level already reached by the great civilization to which they always looked back in

21

9 The rococo ceiling fresco of the monastery of Ottobeuren, Bavaria, showing the Christian emperor Justinian, with St Benedict of Nursia beside him, closing down the Platonic university of Athens in 529

admiration, the civilization of Greece and Rome, nor merely to the level of the great contemporary Asiatic civilizations, of which they had had only a fragmentary, uncomprehending glimpse, but far beyond them, creating ultimately a society unlike anything the world had known before?

For, after all, modern European civilization is not wholly original; nor did it ever, till the eighteenth century, aspire to be original. Most of its ideas had been generated by Antiquity, and particularly by the Greeks. Greek science and technology had continued to advance throughout the period of the Roman Empire, which provided a great

area for the free interchange of goods and ideas. Modern historians have shown that, to the very end of Antiquity, new scientific discoveries were being made. In sixth-century Byzantium, while the Emperor Justinian was closing down the Platonic university of Athens —an episode painted on the ceiling of the great Rococo monastery of Ottobeuren as the last, most glorious triumph of Christianity—neoplatonic scientists, we are told by Professor Sambursky, were anticipating the discoveries of our own time. Other European 'inventions' came from China. It was the Chinese who, in our Dark or Middle Ages, invented gunpowder, printing and the mariner's compass—precisely those three things which, according to Francis Bacon, the prophet of modern scientific thinking, had already by his time 'changed the whole face and state of things throughout the world'. Yet these discoveries, for some reason, were not continued in Byzantium or in China. The Byzantines invented clockwork, of a kind—and how did they use it? To levitate the emperor in order to dazzle the ambassadors of barbarian Europe. The Chinese invented gunpowder, and what did they do with it? They used it, largely, to amuse themselves with firework displays. The Tibetans (I understand from Mr Lynn White) discovered turbine movement; but they were satisfied to exploit it for the rotation of prayer-wheels. Something existed, or something happened, in those mature societies to render their own achievements, from that point onwards, barren. The ideas were there, but the social structure became too soft to sustain them, or too rigid to pursue them. It was western Europe, and western Europe alone, which was able to sustain and pursue them in the cause of further discovery; to make the revolution which those other societies only prepared and made possible.

And why should it be western Europe? Is it not, when we examine the question, rather extraordinary? The trouble about history is that we take it too much for granted. By our explanations, interpretations, assumptions we gradually make it seem automatic, natural, inevitable; we remove from it the sense of wonder, the unpredictability, and therefore the freshness which it ought to have. Who could have predicted in 1910 the incredible events of the last fifty years? Why, then, should we take the course of the past 500 years for granted? History is full of marvels; and although all marvels, to a philosopher, are theoretically capable of explanation, and receive, from scholars, apparently infallible retrospective explanations, that does not make them, in themselves, any less exciting. And surely the rise of western Europe, after its terrible abasement in the Dark Ages, which must at that time have seemed final, far more final than anything we have known since, is a miracle no less fascinating—in spite of all our retrospective efforts at explanation on which we so seldom agree—than the recovery today of China which, like Renaissance Europe, can look back upon a glorious but frustrated Antiquity followed by an inglorious and frustrating Dark Ages.

How did Europe recover? The philosophic historians of the eighteenth century, who first posed the problem, did not ask too many questions of the 'gothic' Middle Ages. To them all those centuries were, more or less, dark centuries: the light broke—literary, cultural, social, economic light—all at once in the fifteenth century, with the 'Revival of Letters'. But I wish, in these pages, to adopt a less wholesale argument. I wish to consider the whole period from the end of the Roman Empire in the West to the Revival of Letters (or, as we would now say, to the Renaissance) not as a static, almost stagnant period in which, to adjust Voltaire's phrase, one barbarian succeeded another on the banks of the Rhine and the Tagus, but as a process; and in that process I wish to single out certain stages, which I think were crucial stages, in the long uneven chain of events whereby the European relics of the deceased Roman Empire were re-animated to become the heart of the modern world.

What are these crucial stages? Every one is complicated by great historical problems: problems of evidence, problems of interpretation, problems of explanation; and it is rash for any man to speak confidently about them, as if they were clear or soluble. How much easier it is merely to narrate the facts which scholars have established, in due chronological order! But since I have undertaken this adventure, let me begin by summarizing the problems which, one after another, will have to be faced. The first is perhaps the greatest, the most insoluble of all. It concerns the end of Antiquity, the decline and dissolution of that great vessel in which its civilization was so long preserved: the Roman Empire.

Why did the Roman Empire decline? Again and again historians and philosophers have asked that question. Its answer, if it could be found, promises to contain the answer to so many other problems which still exercise us today. 'I often wonder', the late Adolf Hitler mused, 'why the Ancient World collapsed'; and he suggested his own answers, which may or may not convince us. He wondered because he too had an interest in empires: he wished to be a new and more successful Augustus whose empire, being free from the fertile seeds of decay—racial impurity, Jewish Christianity—would last for 1,000 years. The fact that even Hitler condescended to wonder, that even he had no cut-and-dried answer, as he had to every other question, illustrates the permanence of the problem: a problem which far profounder thinkers than he had revolved, without resolving, for over 200 years.

Once again, it was in the eighteenth century that men first turned to this great problem of historical explanation. At the beginning of that century Pietro Giannone, the great, unfortunate Neapolitan historian, who exercised a profound influence on all the historians of the Enlightenment, was perplexed by it. In order to find an answer, he dived into the neglected depths of late Roman and Byzantine law. From these legal studies he hoped, as he afterwards wrote, to understand 'the origins and changes of the Roman Empire and how, from its ruins, there arose so many new rulers, laws, customs, kingdoms, and republics in Europe'. Edward Gibbon, profoundly influenced, as he admits, by Giannone, devoted his life to the same problem. As his own great work drew to completion, when, from his study above the lake of Geneva, he could cast his mind back over thirteen centuries and six quarto volumes, he concluded that he had written a history of the triumph of barbarism and religion. He made no secret of his belief that it was the Christians, rather than 'those innocent barbarians', the Goths and Vandals, who had undermined the Empire, just as they had also dilapidated the city of Rome. Many writers, both then and since, have not liked this conclusion. Modern historians have preferred to look for causes in the economy of Rome, or the social structure of the Empire. But as modern historians also see religion as the reflexion and expression of social structure or social ideas, perhaps they do not, after all, differ from Gibbon very profoundly. More recently, a well-known man of letters has remarked, as a truism, that the Roman Empire decayed as the direct result of excessive sexual indulgence. I regret to say that this view, though it has since been taken up with lugubrious zeal by church dignitaries, rests on no discoverable foundations.

But it is not only why the Roman Empire declined that is a mystery to us: it is also when it declined, or rather, when that decline began. The Empire adopted Christianity in the fourth century, but did it not, perhaps thereby, arrest—however temporarily—a decline that had already begun in the military anarchy of the third century: a decline which, at that time, cannot be ascribed to Christianity or even connected with it? So some modern historians date the decline of Rome from a fundamental structural change which took place in the third century, and which the great emperors at the end of that century, and Constantine himself at the beginning of the next, did but stabilize. According to this view there are two successive Roman Empires, even in the West. First, there is the Roman Empire of Augustus and the Antonines, of which we mainly think, the majestic web of planned cities and straight roads, all leading to Rome: the empire whose *Pax Romana*, untroubled by either Barbarians or Christians, extended from the Atlantic to Persia, from the Rhine and the Danube to the Upper Nile and the Sahara. Secondly, after the anarchy of the third century, there is the 'Lower Empire', the rural military empire of Diocletian and Constantine, of Julian the Apostate and Theodosius the Great. This was an empire always on the defensive, whose capital was not Rome, but wherever warring emperors kept their military headquarters: in the Rhineland, behind the Alps or in the East; in Nicomedia or Constantinople, in Trier, Milan or Ravenna.

But even if we agree that the first empire, the familiar pagan empire of the Antonines, underwent its fatal transformation in the third century, before the adoption of Christianity, that does not dispose of the problem. For the second empire, the Christian empire, the last brittle envelope of Greek and Latin Antiquity, also declined and dissolved: and when shall we date its dissolution? Was it in 476 when the barbarian Odoacer deposed the last titular Emperor of the West? Or was it in the sixth century, when the Lombards, pushed forward by the nomadic invaders from the great Steppe that reaches from Russia to China, swept away for ever the briefly restored unity of Rome and Constantinople? Or was it later still, in the seventh century, when the invading Arabs tore away finally—for this surely is one of the great turning-points of history, a moment on which history has never gone back—the Greek provinces of the East from which, for so many centuries, the Roman Empire had drawn its economic, its technical, its cultural sustenance?

The end of Antiquity. that is one great problem which I shall have to consider in these pages. Its effect was enormous: it is one of the great discontinuities of history. It was the end of a whole world, a world which till then had been continuous for over a thousand years. And who could ever have supposed, after it was gone, when its extinction was at last obvious to all—let us say in the eighth century—that Europe could ever recover the position it had once enjoyed, and had now lost? A historical philosopher of the eighth century, if such had existed—some refugee from a former Roman province precariously meditating in a bog in Donegal—might reasonably have concluded that it was all over with Europe: that the torch of civilization had been transferred to other hands, and that, from now on, it was Europe's fate to be a continent of irredeemable barbarians supplying the rich Moslem cities of Baghdad and Cairo and Tunis and Córdoba with iron, skins and slaves.

Yet that imaginary philosopher would have been wrong. Events would prove him wrong; and we must ask why he would have been wrong. What facts, what developments, in the Dark Ages of Europe, gave western society its power of recovery? How was it that Christendom not only recovered but was able, at the end of the eleventh century, to launch a counter-attack? This counter-attack, the Crusades, is surely another of the great turning-points of history. It is the return of Christian Europe to the East with which, under the Roman Empire, it had been united and from which, by the Arab conquests, it had been severed. Indeed, in its limited way—limited in impact, for it bore no universal message, converted no nations; limited in time, for its conquests were transitory—it is the European answer to those conquests.

Not everyone has seen the Crusades in this light. In the eighteenth century David Hume saw them as a 'universal frenzy', an 'epidemic fury' of 'fanatical and romantic warriors', 'the most durable monument of human folly that has yet appeared in any age or nation'. Viewed in isolation, they do indeed seem romantic and quixotic episodes. But when we consider them against the background of the time, and perhaps also when we see them from the vantage-point of the twentieth century, with its epidemic fury of ideological belief, its anti-colonial revolts, they may well appear in a different light. A 'universal frenzy' which launched Europe against Asia, which led to the restoration, after 500 years, of Christian States in the Levant, and the re-creation, in Italy, of commercial cities trading directly with the East, was surely another turning-point, an upward turning-point, just as the Arab conquests had been a downward turning-point, in the history of our continent.

And when we note that the same two centuries which saw the Crusades saw also other forms of European advance which had nothing whatever to do with the Turks or the rescue of the Holy Places—the advance of Spanish Christians against the Moors of Spain, the advance of German settlers against the Slavs in eastern Europe, the conquest of Ireland by the Anglo-Norman barons of England, the conquest of Languedoc by the barons of northern France, and the conquest of Byzantium itself, and all its empire, by Frankish barons and Italian cities, not to speak of new internal institutions—new towns, new religious orders, new universities—we realize that those two centuries were centuries of a general European expansion, and that the Crusades, whether we like them or not, were an inseparable part of that expansion. Perhaps they were no more a 'monument of human folly' than many other great movements which have worn ideological colours: than the Reformation in northern Europe in the sixteenth century or the nationalist movement of the nineteenth or the communist movement of the twentieth.

In fact, the European expansion of the twelfth century did not last. Mysteriously, in the later thirteenth century, Europe began one of its periodic 'declines'. The great efforts of the last two centuries could not be sustained. The conquests in the East were lost. Jerusalem returned to its Moslem, Constantinople to its Byzantine rulers. The advance in the West was stayed. In Spain the Christian Reconquest, which had been so rapid, stood suddenly still. In Ireland the influx ceased and the Anglo-Norman conquerors were absorbed by the natives; they sank into those green bogs and came out talking

Irish, wearing Irish clothes. The Renaissance of the twelfth century died away. The Reformation of the twelfth century—if I may use that term before I explain it—was snuffed out. For another two centuries Europe, Christendom, seemed stagnant. Its wars of conquest and colonization were succeeded by internal wars, civil wars: the Hundred Years' War, the baronial wars, the wars of the Roses, the wars of Burgundians and Armagnacs, the civil wars of Spain and Bohemia, the papal schism. The 200 years between the first and the second Renaissance in Europe, between the age of Dante and Giotto and Marsilio of Padua on the one hand and the age of Savonarola and Leonardo da Vinci and Machiavelli on the other; between the first and second Reformation, between Arnold of Brescia and the Albigensians in the twelfth century and Martin Luther and the Anabaptists in the sixteenth, is an age, in general—of course, there were the inevitable local exceptions—of regression. The break-through, that astonishing break-through of the crusading period, had stopped short. The conquests, the voyages of discovery had ceased. The intellectual speculation was stilled. In the fifteenth century, on the eve of the second Renaissance, Michelet's Renaissance, Burckhardt's Renaissance, *our* Renaissance—for the term has come to stay, however pedants argue—men did not delight in the wonder and freshness of the world. Gone is the calm, confident, extroverted assurance of the statues of the cathedral of Chartres. The new art is, at times, pensive, introspective, even distorted, like the art of the later Baroque age which was also an age of recession, of introversion; the new literature turned to satire, or invective; the new religion to mysticism, to escape.

Why was the European break-through of the twelfth century cut short? What failure in the dynamism, or in the mechanism of society caused it, after two centuries of expansion, to halt again? Is there perhaps a necessary rhythm in such expansion, a time-scale of movement and stability, of rise and fall? Is such a rhythm linked to economic or institutional or demographic changes, or to the mere change of human generations? And why, even more, was the progress so brilliantly resumed in the fifteenth century? For it was then, after nearly two centuries of comparative stagnation, that the

31

life of Europe—whether traditionalists recognized it or not—began to flow again: Prince Henry of Portugal, that almost mythical figure, the solitary of Sagres, sent his fleets on longer and longer journeys to explore the coasts of Africa; the Dukes of Burgundy found themselves sustained, and could in turn sustain their gluttonous, chivalric magnificence, by a new economic prosperity. It was then that the Medici in Florence blossomed from bankers into the most cultivated of princes and the most splendid of popes; then that their successors and supplanters, the Fuggers of Augsburg, rising from cloth-merchants into bankers, found themselves not only financing popes and emperors, who bowed before this new economic leviathan, but creating and commanding a new heavy industry throughout Europe. Before Columbus had sailed to Hispaniola or Bartholomew Dias had discovered the Cape of Good Hope, the society of Europe had already acquired a new strength and a new resilience. Indeed, it was only because it had acquired this new strength that it was able to make and exploit those discoveries. For technical devices, geographical contacts do not of themselves cause the progress of men and nations. Such discoveries are only of service to the societies which are equipped to use them. Often these are the same societies which have been equipped to make them. But it is the equipment, the social and intellectual articulation, not the discoveries, which is the prime cause of the progress which those discoveries do but accentuate or prolong.

These, then, are some of the questions which I must face here. They are large questions, not easily answered. They have provoked learned controversy and been involved in ideological debate. Naturally, in so short a space, I cannot hope to answer them. Perhaps, as Voltaire and other historical philosophers have thought, they are unanswerable. All I can hope and will try to do is, while thinking of them, bearing them always in mind, to speak of certain episodes or periods of history which, in my opinion, represent or illustrate the great turning-points in that remarkable process: the rise of Europe from its eclipse, from the total abasement which followed the fall of the Western Empire of Rome, to the position of strength from which, in the sixteenth century, it set forward to dominate the world.

The end of Antiquity, the final failure of the great Mediterranean civilization of Greece and Rome, is one of the chief problems of European history. Nobody can agree why it happened, or quite when. All that we can see is a slow, fatal, apparently irreversible process which seems to begin in the third century AD and is completed, at least as far as western Europe is concerned, in the fifth. There are periods of recovery, or apparent recovery, between those dates, and there are moments of restoration, even after the last of them. Periodically, during that long decline, great self-made figures, never from Rome, not even from Italy, but from the fringes of the empire, come forward and seek, by heroic efforts, to restore the unity, the security, the stability of the empire. They are famous figures—famous in politics, famous in religion, famous in art —who punctuate the process and give it its dramatic quality: giants who hold up the avalanche, for a time, and whose names and monuments are still legible, or visible, among the debris.

The first of them was Diocletian, the Illyrian peasant—he came from what is now Yugoslavia—who at the end of the third century reorganized the whole empire, put it on a new basis, and then, exhausted by his mountainous labours, retired, like another great overworked emperor, Charles V, and grew cabbages at his native town of Spalato, or Split. Historians see him as the maker of a new age, the founder of a new system. From this accession, in AD 284, they date the foundation of the second Roman Empire: the 'Lower Empire', distinct from the 'Principate' which Augustus had founded and which, after the golden age of the second century, had crumbled in the disasters of the third.

Then there was Constantine the Great, the ablest of Diocletian's immediate successors. Another Illyrian, born at Naissus, or Nish, also now in Yugoslavia, he was raised to the purple at York in 306.

By his double decision to accept Christianity and to build a new, impregnable capital on the Bosphorus, Constantine exercised, perhaps, the greatest influence on western history of any man since Christ. Who can even guess what would have happened to the world, or to Christianity, if the Roman Empire had not become Christian, or if Constantinople had not preserved Roman law and Greek culture through the years of barbarian and Moslem conquest? The rediscovery of Roman law in the twelfth century marked an important stage in the revival of Europe. But the Roman law which was rediscovered was the law preserved in the great Byzantine compilation of Justinian. Similarly, the revival of Greek letters in the fifteenth century made the Renaissance. But Greek letters also had

13 (*Opposite*) The cathedral of Sta Sophia, built by Justinian, was the architectu[?] masterpiece of Constantine's new capital as well as the most splendid expression of acceptance of Christianity. Mohammed II, the Conqueror, converted it into a mosq[?]

11, 12 (*Left*) Diocletian and his Tetrarchy, grim, resolute upholders of the restored empire. (*Right*) One of the defeated: a war-prisoner from a relief on the Arch of Diocletian, Rome

been preserved—such of them as had been preserved—in Byzantium. Without the work of Constantine in founding his new capital it is probable that neither Roman law nor Greek letters would have been there to rediscover, and without his decision to adopt Christianity, Europe might well have accepted some other oriental religion.

Then there is Theodosius the Great, a Spaniard, the first of the Spanish Inquisitors, who at the end of the fourth century carried forward the work of Constantine and made Christianity—and a particular form of Christianity—the official religion of the State. There is something very Spanish about Theodosius. Centuries later, the Spaniards would bash down the pagan idols of Mexico and Peru and demand that all men be made to believe the remarkable doctrine of the Immaculate Conception. Theodosius set fanatical mobs to

bash down the pagan temples of the East and required all his subjects
to believe the no less remarkable doctrine of the Trinity. But behind
this ideological bigotry Theodosius held the Roman Empire
together. He reunited East and West and defended both against
barbarians and usurpers. He was the last great emperor of the West;
and the last recognizably classical Latin poet, the Egyptian Claudian,
shed a kind of twilight lustre over the dynasty which he founded,
the last imperial dynasty of the whole empire.

Finally, a century after all seemed over in the West, there was
Justinian, yet another Illyrian peasant. He too was born in Nish.
What a remarkable race those Illyrians were, who provided the
Roman Empire with three of its greatest emperors! Nor did they
stop there. The greatest of Diocletian's predecessors, the frustrated

14 Late fourth-century silver disc or
missorium of Theodosius the Great
flanked by his two sons, Arcadius and
Honorius

15, 16 The Emperor Justinian as warrior and head of the Church. On the contemporary gold coin, he is preceded by the figure of Victory. In the tenth-century mosaic over the south door of Sta Sophia, he presents the Virgin with his cathedral while Constantine offers his city

beginner of his work, Aurelian, was also an Illyrian; and long after Justinian's death, under their modern name as Albanians, they would provide the Turkish Empire with the greatest of its statesmen and warriors. That Empire too would be sustained and re-created, in its decline, by an 'Illyrian' dynasty of Grand Viziers. But Justinian was not, like most of these Illyrians, a man of great personal stature. He was not a founder, either of a state or of a dynasty. He was a magnificent bureaucrat who slid on to his uncle's throne. If Theodosius

reminds us of a Spanish Inquisitor, Justinian (who was hardly less inquisitorial) reminds us of another magnificent, intolerant, ecclesiastically minded modern ruler, Louis XIV. Once established in power, Justinian reconquered the West, restored the unity of the empire, codified the laws, imported from China into Europe, as his monopoly, the hitherto mysterious manufacture of silk, snuffed out the last relics of paganism; and having thus re-created, as it seemed, the Roman Empire, he left it loaded with majestic churches and ringed

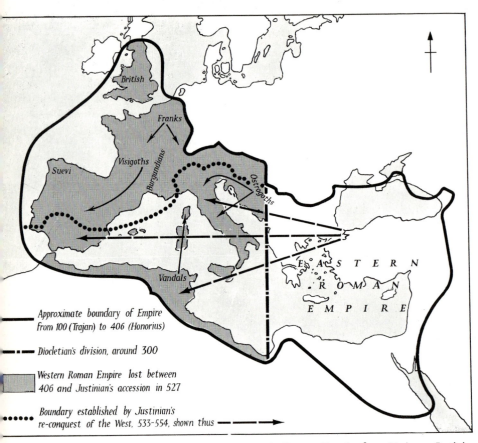

Approximate boundary of Empire
from 100 (Trajan) to 406 (Honorius)

Diocletian's division, around 300

Western Roman Empire lost between
406 and Justinian's accession in 527

Boundary established by Justinian's
re-conquest of the West, 533-554, shown thus

17 The Roman Empire from Trajan to Justinian

by elaborate fortifications. Under Justinian the majesty of Rome shone again, from Spain to the frontiers of Persia, from the Sahara to the Danube. It seemed—superficially at least—as magnificent as ever, secure against all invaders behind its protective Maginot Line.

These are the great figures who dominate the Roman world after the deep structural crisis of the third century. They all have something in common. All of them are hard, ruthless, intolerant, impersonal figures. Most of them were persecutors. Diocletian persecuted the Christians, Theodosius the pagans, Justinian the heretics. Most of them were great builders. Arches and aqueducts, baths and palaces, fortresses and temples commemorate Diocletian, Constantine, Justinian. All of them appear in history, and indeed in art, as men of more than human stature: restless, inexhaustible Titans who contrive, by their huge, devoted efforts, to reverse the fated course of history and prop up, for a time, a remorselessly crumbling edifice. And indeed, as soon as their hand is removed, the edifice does crumble again. Diocletian reorganizes but cannot preserve the pagan empire. When his hand is removed, civil war returns and none can guess the outcome. Constantine gives it a new religion, a new structure, a new dynasty, but cannot inject a new vitality. After his death, it is the old story again: disputed successions, religious differences, Persian victories, barbarian invasions. Theodosius dies, and the empire which he has pulled together splits apart. A year after his death, St Jerome lamented that the whole Roman world was falling and that the Roman army, victor and master of the globe, was helpless before the horsemen of the steppes. Fifteen years later he would learn with horror that Rome itself, the city which had captured the whole world, had been captured by the Goths. Even the spectacular triumphs of Justinian's long reign dissolve with him: after his death Persians, Moslems, barbarians overwhelm his elaborate fortifications; the heretics whom he has persecuted take their revenge by welcoming the conquerors; and at home, in the very capital of the empire, puritan iconoclasts will soon destroy the unbearable magnificence of his churches.

No doubt the impersonal character of the great emperors of the last centuries owes something to the hieratic image given to them by the Church. Early Christian bishops were great flatterers of Christian emperors. Eusebius, bishop of Caesarea, writing about Constantine, or St Chrysostom, writing about Theodosius, are as fulsome as bishop Bossuet on Louis XIV. The Emperor Justinian and his empress Theodora appear, in the mosaics of Ravenna, remote stylized figures: who would guess from those severe postures that the empress had been a prostitute, practising rather more flexible postures on the stage? It is appropriate that the only emperor of those

centuries who seems human to us is the pagan, Julian the Apostate, who had the advantage of a sympathetic pagan historian. But this is not a complete explanation. After all, Julian too, human though he is, appears to us as a man swimming vainly against an irresistible current. In advance, he saw himself as such. When he was invested with the purple he saw it as a kind of condemnation to death: he was heard quietly quoting to himself a line of Homer about 'purple death and overmastering fate'. His attempt to restore the old paganism was as vain as the attempts of his rivals to re-animate the empire by christianizing it. His paganism was anyway somewhat spurious. It was not really the old humane paganism of Greece but a superstitious modern variant of it. After his death, all that he had done

18 Justinian's empress, Theodora, with her attendants. (Contemporary mosaic from the church of San Vitale, Ravenna)

19 Julian 'the Apostate', the restorer of paganism: an approachable, human figure in a succession of impersonal emperors

crumbled, and his last words, we are told, were: *'vicisti Galilaee'*— Man of Galilee, you have won.

How are we to explain this apparently irreversible decline of the Roman Empire, a decline against which, as it seemed, no human effort, no political genius, could prevail? It is rash to suggest any general cause for any historical problem, and especially for a problem of this magnitude. But let me point to a few of the major factors which historians have studied and in which, or in whose combination, part at least of the explanation may lie. These major factors are three. The first of them is the relationship between town and country; the second is the religion of the State; the third is the barbarian invasions.

43

20, 21, 22 Regular, central planning and imposing public buildings: (*opposite*) aerial view of Timgad, Algeria; (*this page, top and centre*) baths at Timgad and the amphitheatre at Arles

23, 24 Architecture on the Greek model: triumphal arch at Palmyra, Syria (*opposite, bottom left*) and, in the adjacent illustration, remains of the temple of Jupiter at Baalbek

25 The Porta Nigra at Trier, Germany, one of the largest cities in the Western Empire and for a time its capital

The problem of town and country in the Roman Empire has long exercised historians. It is unquestionable that the decline of the towns, and the ruralization of Europe, played a large part in the gradual inner transformation which robbed the Empire of its old strength. For the Roman Empire, in its great days, in the golden 'age of the Antonines'—the period from Trajan to Marcus Aurelius, which men afterwards regarded as the happiest era in the history of mankind—had been essentially a civilization of cities. Those magnificent, well-planned cities whose remains are so well known to us, with their paved streets and municipal buildings, their theatres and temples, law-courts and public baths, still seem to us the essence of Roman civilization. Imposing, centrally planned, regularly laid out, they convey a vivid impression of order, uniformity, authority. They are very different from the medieval cities of Europe. They did not grow up accidentally; there was nothing higgledy-piggledy about them; they are not the result of a confluence of merchants clustering round a castle or a monastery. They are laid out and laid down from above. They are *founded* cities, often imperially founded, as their names make clear: Caesarea, Augusta, Adrianople, Constantinople. The names of the emperors which they bear give them a public, official character which their public official monuments still conserve, making them, whether they are in Europe, Asia or Africa, permanently 'Roman'.

At least we call them 'Roman'. But when we look closer, we soon see that their genealogy is not Roman. Rome, republican Rome, is not a model for them. Like so much in the Roman Empire, their model is not Italian, not even European, but eastern. They have their origin, for the most part, in other founded cities—Philippi, Alexandria, Antioch, Seleucia, Ptolemais: the Greek cities placed all around the eastern Mediterranean by its Macedonian conquerors. We naturally think of the Empire founded by Augustus as the Roman Empire. It was Roman arms which conquered it; the Caesars, who founded its institutions, were Roman; and Rome was its capital. But in fact Rome was not its natural centre of gravity. The wealth which sustained it came largely from Asia and Africa, and particularly from the East. Africa supplied the city of Rome with two-thirds of its corn. It was the conquest of Egypt which enabled Augustus to establish the Empire, the tribute of eastern provinces which kept it going. And increasingly it was in the Greek cities of the East that its culture lay, thence that its competing new religions came.

At a very early date the artificiality of rule from Rome was shown. Already before the 'age of the Antonines' it had been discovered, as Tacitus remarked, that emperors could be made elsewhere than at Rome. By the third century AD they were generally made elsewhere. In that century there were not only military usurpers from the frontier: there were also Syrian, African and half-barbarian emperors; and their visits to Rome became rarer and rarer. By the fourth century the city of Rome was a historic backwater. Its sack by the Goths under Alaric in 410 was, of course, a great emotional shock. I have mentioned the shock that it gave to St Jerome in Palestine. Rome after all was still Rome, the immortal, impregnable city, the city which had eluded the Gauls and defied even Hannibal. Such a shock caused men to doubt the divine basis of the empire. The pagans said that it was the adoption of Christianity which had caused the disaster, and St Augustine wrote his most famous work, *The City of God*, to refute them. But it was not a real disaster; for by then the capital had long lain elsewhere. The capital, being the headquarters of a military emperor, was in the North, within reach of the threatened northern frontiers, the Danube and the Rhine. It was in Nicomedia, in Constantinople, in Ravenna, in Milan, in Trier.

If the centre of government lay in the North, away from Rome, the centres of culture were equally far from Rome, in the East. The philosophical schools were in Athens, the law schools in Beirut. Science was studied in Egypt and Syria. It was in Egypt that Ptolemy mapped the heavens as Eratosthenes had once measured the earth. The great school of technology, the great library of learning were in Alexandria. After AD 200, the most famous writers of the empire came from the Greek cities of the East—even those, like the historian Ammianus or the poet Claudian, who wrote in Latin; the great westerners—Tertullian, Apuleius, Augustine—came from Africa. And the economic centre of the empire was in those Greek or hellenized eastern cities too. Two-thirds of its population lived in the

27 The Pont du Gard, near Nîmes. Built about AD 14, this greatest of all Roman aqueducts carried water along the top tier of arches, some 180 feet above the river

26 Roman funeral monument from Neumagen on the lower Rhine, in the form of a wine-carrying ship. It probably commemorated one of the wealthy city merchants who acquired control of the rich vineyards in this area

eastern provinces. Those provinces, with Africa, produced the corn for Italy and for the imperial armies. They were also the commercial and industrial heart of the empire. Through them, by sea and caravan, passed the long-distance trade which fed it with silk from China and spices from Indonesia. In them the manufactured goods were produced for export to the western provinces: Syrian and Jewish merchants carried them to Spain, France, Britain. And the taxes levied on their wealth, eastern wealth, sustained the great, overworked machine of government and war.

Very different were the Roman cities of the West—Segovia, Merida, Arles, Cologne, York. They were military camps, strategic posts, vital crossroads. As such they were mainly consuming, not producing cities. Those of them which produced were agricultural

centres. They produced not corn—corn was better grown in North Africa—but oil and wine: especially wine. Some of the most famous vineyards of today are grouped round the Gallo-Roman cities of the Empire—Reims, the capital of champagne, Trier the capital of the empire itself. Our vineyards, writes a French historian, 'are a Roman monument, one of the best preserved Roman monuments in our country'. If they did not grow up round Roman cities, they grew up round their successors, those episcopal cities which prolonged the structure and articulation of the Roman Empire into the Middle Ages.

Thus if the Roman Empire is a vast federation of cities—majestic cities linked by majestic roads—there is a great difference between the cities of the East and of the West. The eastern cities are real cities.

They produced the wealth which sustains the empire. The western cities are colonial cities: they live on the surplus of the East, which comes to them through taxation, and on the manufactures of the East, bought with the yield of taxes or by the sale of their wine and oil. Superficially, the cities may look the same: all have their amphitheatres, their forums, their baths. But structurally there is a difference. The East is still, as in the days before the Roman conquest, an urban civilization. The West is still rural, a provincial, even a colonial society. We see the difference in their culture. The famous literary figures of the East are professors, theologians, advocates, scientists, the products of a sophisticated urban society. Those of the West, even in Italy, are great rural landlords or Roman officials: often both.

So much for the cities, but what about the country? Naturally enough, we know less about the country; but one thing, I think, is fairly clear. The more sophisticated the cities, the less contact they had with the country around them. In Asia, in Egypt, the cities were Greek, but the countries were Egyptian, Syrian, Anatolian. In north-west Africa, in Spain, in Gaul and in Britain the cities were

28 Gallic peasant taking his produce to market, from a first-century marble relief

Roman, the countries Punic, Berber, Iberian, Celtic. Members of the once conquered peoples—they were all Roman citizens now—were absorbed into the cities and, if rich enough, adapted themselves to the city culture; but the difference remained. And anyway, what was this city culture? The very fact that the cities were imposed on the country, founded and peopled by the conquerors, rather than growing out of them, made their culture somewhat artificial. It was a polite, traditional, cosmopolitan Greco-Roman culture for a leisured, governing, tax-consuming class. It meant little to the native artisans and crowded poor of the great cities of the East; less to the native peasants of the surrounding countryside who retained their old idioms, their old habits, their old religious cults. Only in the cities had these cults been fully amalgamated with the formal, established, imperially consecrated worship of Greece and Rome.

All through the golden age of the Antonines, while the structure of the empire remained sound, it was based on the cities. Cultivated Roman governors, representing at their best, like the Antonine emperors themselves, Roman gravity and Stoic principles, presided over an orderly, cultivated urban society. Rich tourists travelled from

29 Peasants paying money, perhaps rent, to a city man, assisted by his clerks. (Early third-century relief from Neumagen)

city to city, headed by the emperor Hadrian himself, that indefatigable globe-trotter, whose name is commemorated in Newcastle-upon-Tyne, in Jerusalem, in Adrianople. We get numerous glimpses of Hadrian on his travels, striding out on foot, ahead of his panting courtiers, to inspect the historic sites of his vast empire; and of course the imperial example was widely followed. An industrious Greek Baedeker, one Pausanias, wrote an indispensable guide-book for such Hellenic travellers, and out of the urban poor there emerged to oblige them a class of professional guides whose fundamental ignorance and ready invention were maddening to the connoisseur. Such travel strengthened the cosmopolitanism of a cosmopolitan empire. It also strengthened the cosmopolitan ruling class. In North

30 Hadrian's Wall, built in AD 121–6 as a barrier against the Picts of Scotland, fenced the northern limit of his empire with a triple line of defence over 75 miles long. The massive stone wall, about 10 ft thick and 15 ft high, is protected on each side by a ditch

Africa, in Asia, in Europe the Greco-Roman establishment entrenched itself comfortably in the cities. Deep down into urban society it thrust its roots. For its sustenance it collected rents and taxes. For it, eastern trade was organized. For it, local manufactures were developed. And the unestablished world—rural and urban, peasant and artisan—ranged itself in due subordination, accepting its superiority, competing for its patronage, for it seemed permanent.

But in fact it was not permanent. In times of prosperity a tax-consuming, *Tatler* class may be quietly accepted: it provides employment; it may even provide leadership. But in an economic crisis its weak foundations are exposed. In the middle of the third century AD an economic crisis struck the empire. What exactly caused it we

31 Contemporary marble portrait-bust of the Emperor Hadrian, who personally visited the farthest frontiers of his empire

do not know. There was a long political crisis: a perpetual struggle for the throne. There were foreign pressures: the barbarians began to press on the Rhine and the Danube; under its new Sassanian kings, Persia became a formidable rival to Rome. But mere political and military threats seldom cause fundamental crises in society; more often they only reveal them. The crisis of the empire in the third century was not merely in the capital: who should be emperor; nor on the frontiers: how to keep Goths and Gepids and Persians at bay; it was in the body of the empire. Dreadful plagues (plagues can be of decisive importance in history) were brought in by the barbarians, decimating the population—and then the barbarians themselves had to be admitted to fill the gaps. Even so, the population of the empire shrank. It is said to have shrunk by a third. This naturally affected the strength of the army and the produce of industry. At the same time the supply of gold failed. Why it failed we do not know. Some say the European mines gave out; others that the continual adverse balance of trade drained it away to the East. More probably it was the economic stimulus—the delicate commercial machinery of production—which fainted. At all events, without gold to export, the long-distance trade with the East languished. With trade, the currency too collapsed, and with it the fixed revenue of the State. It was a vicious spiral of decline which could not be checked by emperors uncertain of their title and preoccupied, in their short reigns, by civil and foreign war.

This crisis of the third century produced some odd emperors. At one time a Syrian priest, at another a Thracian pugilist sat on the throne once occupied by Trajan and Marcus Aurelius. Some emperors secured the throne by murder; one bought it outright for cash. There were some terrible humiliations. The worst was the defeat and capture of the Emperor Valerian by the Persians. A Sassanian rock-carving above the old Persian capital of Persepolis commemorates this famous scene. For the emperor it was a permanent humiliation; for the rest of his life he was carried about in chains to be a living footstool for the Persian king when he mounted his horse. No such indignity befell any other emperor till the ninth century, when the dreadful Bulgarian Khan Krum, having defeated

32 The Sassanian rock-carving commemorating the victories of the Persian king Sapor I. The emperor Valerian, captured at Edessa in 259, is held by the wrist; kneeling in supplication is Philip the Arab, while beneath the horse's feet lies Gordian III, killed by his own troops

and killed one of the ablest of Byzantine rulers, converted his skull into a drinking-cup for use in merry barbarian potations.

These were dramatic episodes in the disintegration of the first Roman Empire, the Empire of the Caesars and the Antonines. Less dramatic, but ultimately more significant, were the accompanying changes in town and country, in the religion and the army of State. For when economic crisis fell on those great Roman towns, the precariousness of their Greco-Roman ruling class became clear. Within the towns, that class found itself without influence among the independent artisans and the poor. Outside, it was without influence in the countryside. The urban poor showed their estrangement by taking to new religions. Leaving the privileged classes to bow before the now bloodless gods of their tradition, or to parade the uncommitted stoic and epicurean virtues—virtues which might help the individual to walk self-contained and imperturbable through the uncertainties of life but could provide no cement to a tottering society—they turned aside to the warmer, more mysterious new heresies of the East which, like Methodism in eighteenth-century England, offered to a whole community of believers a more positive consolation and a more complete salvation. At the same time the rural poor turned aside too. In the years of distress, when their foreign masters seemed to have lost the secret of government, they remembered their older, national identity. Recalling that they were not Greeks or Romans, but Syrians, Egyptians, Berbers, they remained aloof and indifferent, resentful but powerless—unless they were mobilized, as many of them were, in the army.

Thus the third century, that most critical century of the empire, saw first the economic decline, then the isolation and eclipse of those Greco-Roman urban oligarchies which hitherto, in effect, had governed, indeed been, the empire. The emperors of that century who, in the absence of a hereditary system, had fought or bought their way to power, had necessarily relied on the army. Once in power, they might turn to the town oligarchies for support; but the support they could find there was feeble. Food from the country was now more important to maintain the army than taxes in debased currency—and anyway, few of those emperors lasted long enough to enjoy urban support, if they had won it. Before long a new usurper would make his rival appeal to the army and to the enemies of the towns. And in appealing away from the urban establishment, these ambitious new rulers appealed, inevitably, to the new heresies; the heresies which pullulated in the underworld of the cities and which now, in the instability of the cities, were coming into their own.

So we come to one of the most fascinating developments of the later Roman Empire: the rise of the new 'mystery religions'. Since these new religions arose in the underworld of the cities, and since the great cities of the empire were largely in the East, they were, naturally enough, eastern religions. Or rather, they were eastern heresies. For it is seldom that the official religion of one country becomes popular in another civilized state: that smacks too much of 'cultural imperialism'. What is accepted, in such circumstances, is not the orthodoxy but the heresy of neighbouring powers; and so the new religions which found acceptance in the Roman Empire were often variants of the established religions of the East.

Some of these new 'mystery religions', at one time the most attractive of them, were Persian. For in the Persian Empire, the great rival of Rome, the ruling class had also adopted a rigid archaic traditionalism, and in the towns of Persia the suppressed, resentful classes had listened to new heresies which the kings of Persia, in times of need, had sometimes seemed to favour. In the third and fourth centuries two of these Persian heresies penetrated the Roman Empire and achieved spectacular diffusion. They were Mithraism and Manichaeism. Mithraism was the heresy of the western fringes of the old Persian Empire, where the orthodoxy of Zoroaster mingled with the older religions of Syria. With its new cult of purity and its ritual slaughter of bulls to wash away the sins of the world, it was carried by Roman soldiers to their camps on the Rhine and Danube, in Brittany and in Spain, London and Hadrian's Wall. Manichaeism was the gospel of the Persian teacher Mani, who was crucified for it in AD 276. He saw the world as a struggle between the equally balanced forces of Good and Evil, and his ideas, which were to have a long and colourful history in Europe and Asia, would tempt the powerful imagination of St Augustine in the great worldly city of Carthage in Tunisia. Several Roman emperors felt that, to re-stabilize their shaken empire, they must copy the Persians who had so successfully restabilized theirs: they must invest the throne with Persian ceremonial, adopt Persian rites, accept a Persian religion—or rather, since the Persian orthodoxy was inseparable from the Persian State, a Persian heresy.

But there were also Egyptian and Syrian heresies which at times were very popular. The new synthetic Egyptian god Serapis—an invention of the Greek kings of Egypt, the Ptolemies—had made early conquests in the empire. So had his female colleague Isis. Both of them had temples in Italy and Gaul, and on the frontiers of the empire in Europe and Africa. In the second century AD the sophisticated African writer Apuleius was one of those who were captivated by the warm, mystical devotion of Isis. And how can anyone avoid quoting Gibbon's account of the attempt by the Syrian emperor Elagabalus to establish in Rome the Syrian sun god of whom he was the priest? When the temple of the new god was ceremonially installed on the Palatine mount, says the historian, 'the richest wines, the most extraordinary victims, and the rarest aromatics were consumed on his altar; around the altar a chorus of Syrian damsels performed their lascivious dances to the sound of barbarian music, whilst the gravest personages of the state and army, clothed in long Phoenician tunics, officiated in the meanest functions, with affected zeal and secret indignation.' Another of these oriental mystery-religions was Christianity which, in the time of Nero, had been preached by St Paul to the urban poor of the eastern cities, Salonika, Corinth, Colossae, Ephesus, and in Rome itself. But nothing in the third century suggested that this Jewish heresy could rival the more tempting mystery-religions of Persia, Syria or Egypt.

So all through the third century we see a consistent process. The old ruling class of the empire, the city oligarchies of the East, together with its culture and its religion, the established Greco-Roman paganism, is in decline. The urban poor, the rural classes, have no interest in that artificial society which can no longer justify itself by prosperity and which has lost confidence in itself. Nor has the army any natural loyalty towards the cities which, more and more, are becoming detached from it. Why should an army recruited from peasants and, increasingly, from European barbarians precariously settled on the fringes of the empire, feel loyalty to distant Asiatic and African cities whose way of life is so different from its own? Moreover, in the third century the army was more necessary than ever. It was necessary to the emperors in order to secure power. It was necessary to the empire in order to deal with provincial revolt and barbarian invasion. And because it was so necessary it had the self-confidence which the inessential, parasitic class of town magnates was beginning to lose.

33, 34 Two Persian religions which competed with Christianity for domination of the Roman world: (*above*) Mithraism, whose god Mithras washed away the sins of the world with the ritual sacrifice of bulls; (*below*) Manichaeism: this fresco, supposedly of Mani and his followers, comes from the oasis of Turfan in Sinkiang

35, 36 Egyptian rivals of Christ: late second-century head of Serapis and (*centre*) the worship of Isis. In this fresco at Herculaneum the morning service of opening the temple is being performed at a sanctuary in Campania

37 (*Right*) 'Syncretism': in the late Roman Empire the rival new religions were often fused together. This mosaic from the ancient mausoleum beneath St Peter's, Rome, shows Christ with the attributes of the pagan Sun-god

Such was the problem of the Roman Empire in the third century of its existence. At the end of that century a solution was found. By turning away from the towns and placing their first interest squarely in the army, a series of emperors contrived to defend the frontiers, to ward off the barbarians. But they failed to solve the internal problems of the empire. They imposed ever heavier burdens on the towns, thus hastening their decline. They struggled with the new religions, but could give no strength to the old. The greatest of them, Diocletian, decided to follow the Persian example. Discarding the forms of ancient liberty which Augustus had carefully preserved, and which had satisfied the traditional ideas of Roman senators and Greek citizens, he surrounded his throne with oriental pomp, oriental servility: an elaborate hierarchy, a court nobility, a tribe of eunuchs. He also accepted one of the new Persian heresies. In A D 307, when Constantine was already one of his junior partners in government, he solemnly declared Mithras the protector of the empire. From that moment Mithraism might have become the religion of Rome. Had it done so, the pagan ceremonies which so quickly crystallized round the teaching of Christ would no doubt have accommodated themselves instead to the cult of Mithras, and the *taurobolium*, the baptism with bull's blood in underground caves, would have replaced the crucifixion and the sacrament of the Last Supper at the centre of European worship.

As he inclined towards one heresy, Diocletian persecuted the others which he did not choose. In particular, he persecuted Christians. It was the great persecution of the years 303–312, famous in the annals of our Church. But in persecuting the Christians, Diocletian—or rather his successors who were the real movers and the continuators of the persecution—soon discovered an important fact. Since the last persecution—the persecution of Decius in the middle of the third century—Christianity had acquired a new strength. I have mentioned that all the new heresies had begun in the towns. Most of them had remained in the towns. Some—in particular Mithraism— had been taken up by the army. But in recent years Christianity, and only Christianity, had, in wide and important areas, conquered the country. Thanks to that conquest it had acquired a new toughness

38 Thirteenth-century frescoes illustrating Constantine's alleged surrender of his temporal power in the West to Pope Sylvester, first claimed by the papacy in the eighth century. Supported by forged documents, the 'Donation of Constantine' was not disproved until the fifteenth

which was proof against persecution. Like Calvinism in seventeenth-century Scotland, or in the 'Desert' of southern France, it was preserved, even when its leaders faltered, by an obstinate, puritan peasantry. With such a base, it could not be stamped out.

So when Constantine, after a bloody civil war, gathered up again the inheritance of Diocletian, he did not stop where Diocletian had stopped. He went one stage further. From Diocletian he accepted a military monarchy, absolute, hierarchical, hereditary, oriental, on the Persian model: drawing its strength from the country, not merely from the towns whose old privileges were now crushed. Like Diocletian, he fixed his capital in the East, the real centre of the empire. Diocletian had reigned in Nicomedia, on the sea of Marmora; Constantine chose a near-by city on the Bosphorus: Byzantium. Like Diocletian he sought to stabilize the currency, and did so far more effectively. Like Diocletian, he turned aside from the old pagan orthodoxy. But the new eastern religion which he chose was not Syrian or Persian or Egyptian: it was the religion which had shown itself to be a force in the country. By his conversion (whatever his motives), by identifying the empire with Christianity, Constantine took the last logical step in shifting its basis away from the now effete urban aristocracies. From now on the monarchy was stabilized on an increasingly Christian, increasingly rural base.

63

The increasingly rural character of the Christian empire after Constantine is well known. It was not the consequence of Christianity; Christianity, after all, had begun as a town movement. But Christianity was an evangelical religion: it had not contented itself with the towns, it had gone out and conquered the country. And now it drew its greatest strength—a new, puritan, messianic strength—from the country. It was in the rural Kabyle area of Algeria—a centre of Moslem puritanism long afterwards, a centre of revolt even today—that a puritan movement of the fourth century threatened to disrupt the unpuritan, over-compliant state Church. It was among the peasants of Egypt and Syria that Christianity was spread by the strange new tribe of monks and hermits, whose antics make such enjoyable reading: St Antony with his delicious temptations; St Pachomius with his unappetizing fare of dried palm-leaves; St Simeon Stylites on his aerial obelisk. And many of these monks and hermits, like many of their rural converts, had fled into the country from the towns: those towns which were now doubly taxed to sustain the heavy cost of the new empire. The most spectacular of such hermits, the man who was to become the patron and pattern of hermits in the Middle Ages, was St Jerome: that learned, metropolitan, epicurean man of letters who made monasticism fashionable by retiring from Rome itself and setting up, with a company of rich and fashionable female penitents, in the desert of Palestine. 'To me', wrote Jerome, 'the town is a prison, solitude is a paradise'; and he preached, in magnificent, ornate, classical prose, a gospel of austere, unmusical, unwashed, sexless puritanism.

The Christian conquest of the country is but one aspect of a larger movement. By the end of the fourth century town-life in general was losing its charm. The old cities of the empire were sunk in their commerce. Merchants were going out of business, going away. The local magistrates, forced to raise the same taxes from a dwindling and impoverished people, were refusing their ungrateful offices. In order to prevent further evasion, the emperor responded by making all unpopular offices hereditary and sought to compel service. In the end, the magistrates themselves, in despair, preferred to flee. Like so many townsmen, they fled into the country, to the protection of

39, 40 The founders of desert monasticism:
details from *The Temptation of St Antony (left)* and *St Jerome in the Desert*,
both by the Flemish painter Hieronymus Bosch

great rural landlords who, in that century, vastly increased their power.

It was in the already rural West, naturally enough, that this process went farthest. In Italy and Gaul, in the last century of the Western Empire, we catch glimpses of the life of the new great landlords who seem isolated, stable giants in a foundering world. Most of them, of course, were inarticulate; many of them were romanized Goths or Gauls; but some of them chose to illustrate their wealth and flavour their power with the faded remnants of the old polite letters of Greco-Roman society. Such, in the fourth century, was Symmachus, a great Roman aristocrat and rural *grand seigneur*: one of the last great patrons of literary paganism. To the *canaille* of Rome he gave (as he claimed) the grandest, most expensive games ever given—how tiresome, he sighed, that a large number of exotic barbarians, whom he had fetched at great cost to exhibit, died on the journey! To maintain his rural *ménage*, he asked a friend on the Danube to send him twenty slaves as stable-boys—the supply, he explained, was better and cheaper on the frontier. And in the intervals of extracting and spending the profits of rural serfdom, he wrote elaborate letters, full of literary affectation, empty of intellectual substance. In the next century Sidonius Apollinaris lived a somewhat similar, if more precarious life in Gaul, in the Auvergne. Around him society was violent and insecure. He describes the invasion of barbarians: Vandals and Huns and Burgundians with buttered hair. But his own life was stable enough: a life of house-parties, tennis-parties, swimming-parties and delicious dinner-parties. For Sidonius too was a great landlord. As son-in-law of one of the last shadowy emperors of the West, he moved in the highest Gallo-Roman society, and described the magnificence of barbarian courts; and on an appropriate occasion he converted himself, without inconvenient change of residence or undignified spiritual struggle, from a great, complacent, senatorial landlord into a bishop of his diocese.

If we put these various processes together, we can see, I think, what is happening. That half-century of political anarchy, from AD 250 to 300, combined with depopulation, pestilence, and the failure of those gold-supplies which were the motor of long-distance trade, has fatally weakened the old, urban economy of the empire. As a military empire, obliged to defend itself on all frontiers and against usurpation at home, its most pressing need was to feed its armies, and if wealth from commerce failed, direct contributions from the land became more and more necessary. So the towns were crushed under higher taxes, commerce was caught in a descending spiral, and the terms shifted between country and town. The impoverishment of the towns weakened the old pagan ruling class and strengthened the outsiders, the heretics. In particular, it strengthened the Christians, whose proselytizing zeal and highly organized charitable relief now found full scope. The direct dependence on the country strengthened the great landlords. This general process was happening anyway. The more the army was needed, the more the process was hastened. In the end, faced by anarchy at the centre, revolts in the provinces, barbarian pressure, and the Persian revival, the great Illyrian emperors—Diocletian and Constantine—decided to take it as *datum*. Their reorganization can be seen as recognition and rationalization of the new facts against which their predecessors had vainly striven. They shifted the capital of the empire to its real economic base, the East. They rested the government squarely on rural, not urban support. They stabilized the currency at a lower level. And to consecrate their work they accepted a new religion of state.

All this, it is clear, has little to do with the third force which I have mentioned, the invasions of 'those innocent barbarians' (as Gibbon called them) who are so often credited with the ruin of Rome. In fact, it is clear, they did not ruin it: indeed, in some respects we may say that the barbarians preserved rather than destroyed the Empire. They filled the gaps in its population and became its defenders. By the third century the Roman armies were largely manned by barbarians—*barbarus* is now the ordinary Latin word for 'soldier'. Barbarians rise high in the imperial service: we think of Stilicho, the romanized Vandal who sustained the burden of the Western empire when Theodosius the Great was dead. And even after the Western Empire had dissolved—when the imperial power had contracted to what had always been its economic basis, the rich if dwindling cities of the East, and the rural Western Empire, unable to sustain itself alone, had shrivelled away—the same process continues. The barbarians do not destroy the empire; they do not think of destroying it; they continue it, or think that they are continuing it. The barbarian Christian kings who rule over Italy, France, Spain in the fifth and sixth centuries still regard themselves as Roman; though they have abolished what Gibbon called 'the useless and expensive office' of Western emperor, they still acknowledge themselves subject to the emperor in the East; they still respect Roman traditions, Roman methods. In the sixth century, when Theodoric the Ostrogoth rules as king of Italy from the former imperial capital of Ravenna, three great Italian figures seem still to represent the old historic Rome. The senator Boethius, who sought to reconcile Plato and Aristotle and whose *Consolation of Philosophy* was translated by our King Alfred and Chaucer, could be seen by Gibbon as the worthy heir of Cicero; Cassiodorus, who founded the tradition of monastic learning in the rural solitude of Squillace in Calabria, recalls Cicero's disputations at the villa of Tusculum; and St Benedict of Nursia, the founder of western monasticism, who created, for an atomized rural society, the basic social and economic cell of its survival—the little religious community living without money on co-operative production of corn, wine and oil—can be seen by Dr Knowles, thanks to his emphasis on gravity, stability, authority and moderation, as 'one of the last of the Romans': the embodiment, in an age of shifting landmarks and peoples, of all the oldest Roman virtues.

41 The typical monastery was a self-sufficient rural community. Its produce included fish bred in the *vivarium* illustrated here

This theoretical and emotional continuity of Rome, even when the western part of the Empire was ruralized beyond the capacity of self-defence, this reassertion, in Gothic Italy, of the old Roman identity, was what would give plausibility to Justinian's attempt to reunite the Empire in the sixth century. To us, looking at it in retrospect, that attempt seems belated, doomed to failure. Were not the barbarians already in power throughout the West? Was not the fatal date already past? But to Justinian, at the time, it did not seem too late. Why should it? When he looked around him, or looked back, he saw no irreversible cataclysm, no dark age. On the contrary, he saw the Roman world. It had been shaken indeed, terribly shaken, but not shattered; and it could be restored. The separate imperial court in the West had shrivelled away. The barbarians had imposed their temporary rule. But all this was very recent. Justinian was but three years younger than Boethius, Cassiodorus and St Benedict, all three of whom had been born in the same year; and he felt himself no less Roman than they. Latin, not Greek, was his native language, and even in the Greek city of Constantinople he liked to emphasize it. His great code of law was written mainly in Latin: only the last, most modern part of it, the *Novellae*, did he suffer to appear exclusively in Greek. He felt himself to be no less Roman than Diocletian, Constantine and Theodosius, who also, whatever concessions they made to their eastern provinces, insisted that they were the heirs not of Alexander but of Augustus.

Thus in 527, when Justinian succeeded to sole power in Byzantium, his duty and his opportunity seemed clear. There was no Western emperor. Theodoric had just died. There was a vacancy of power in the West. What more natural than to fill it by restoring the empire of Theodosius? So, from the natural capital of the empire, Constantinople, still fed by the tribute of the East, Justinian would reach out to recover the separated provinces. From his foothold in Ravenna, the capital of Theodosius' children, the capital of Odoacer and of Theodoric, he would claim the secular and spiritual primacy of the West. To emphasize his claims he would build there a series of new, defiant, magnificent churches: those marvellous churches of Ravenna which preserve his image today. Thanks to two great generals, Belisarius and Narses, he would destroy Gothic rule in Italy, conquer North Africa and part of Spain. Old Rome, in the last century, had lost control of the sea to the Vandals: the final collapse of the Western Empire had been heralded when the Vandal king Genseric had sailed from Carthage and captured the city of Rome itself. It had been a fourth Punic war, a revenge for Hannibal. But now all that was reversed. The Vandals, like the Goths, were overthrown and the Mediterranean would once again, under Justinian, become a 'Roman' lake.

But not for long. In the century after Justinian's death a new blow would fall, and this time the blow would not be delivered against the less essential, rural provinces of the West. It would not be delivered by already romanized, or half-romanized barbarians. It would come from the East and it would be delivered at the real heart of the Roman Empire in the East, in Africa, and later on the sea. Hitherto we have seen the western provinces of Rome sustained, defended, lost and recovered from the East; but the eastern base of the Empire had remained sound. Rome and Persia might bang away at each other—they banged away for 400 years—but neither could ever destroy the other: only their common frontiers shifted slightly as the balance of war wavered. But a day would come when a new force would arise in the East, and the 400-year-old dynasty of Persia and the 1,000-year-old state religion of Persia would be destroyed for ever. Nor would Rome benefit by the ruin of her ancient enemy. Antioch and Alexandria, the greatest Greek cities in the East, with the richest provinces of the empire, would be lost to Byzantium and Christendom. Byzantium itself would be nearly conquered. With those losses, the original economic basis of the united Roman Empire would disappear: that empire would shrink into a precarious society poised on the shores of the Aegean and the Black Sea, irrelevant to western Europe; and western Europe, inheriting from the empire only the state religion of Constantine and the accidental religious primacy of the Bishop of Rome, would be left to find its own way out of the darkness as best it could.

Twenty-five years ago there was published, posthumously, the last work of one of the greatest of European historians, Henri Pirenne. It was a book about the transformation of Europe between the fall of the Roman Empire in the West and the coming of feudalism, and on this subject it advanced a thesis of beautiful simplicity and profound learning which historians have discussed ever since. Its title revealed something of its wide scope and defiant clarity. It was called *Mahomet and Charlemagne*.

Pirenne's thesis can be summarized very briefly. First he asked, when did the real break come? The conventional date was AD 476, the year in which the last Western emperor, Romulus Augustulus, was deposed by the barbarian Odoacer. But, replied Pirenne, this was merely a political event, the end of a political system. It did not affect the social structure of the later Roman Empire, which continued, disintegrating indeed but essentially unchanged, for another 200 years or more. Look at the barbarian kings of the sixth and seventh centuries—Visigoths in Spain, Ostrogoths in Italy, Franks and Germans. They use Roman methods, Roman titles. If they have abolished the shadowy empire in the West, it is not to create a barbarian empire in its place, for they still regard themselves as subjects of the real emperor whose prerogative—at a distance—they respect. Only that emperor, they insist, is in Constantinople, in the East. That is the real seat of power: there is no need of an additional emperor in the rural West. This, we have seen, was not a revolutionary doctrine. It was simply the final recognition of a long-concealed social fact; a fact which Justinian, in the sixth century, sought to emphasize in politics too.

At what point, then, did the real break occur? Pirenne argued that it occurred much later, over a hundred years after the death of Justinian, in the eighth century; and he illustrated his point by looking

71

for significant economic changes. In particular, he examined certain luxury commodities which had circulated in the Roman Empire: gold, silk, papyrus and spices. Gold had been mined in Roman Europe and was exported to the East in exchange for Asiatic luxuries, especially Chinese silk and Indonesian spices. Papyrus came from Egypt. All these exotic goods were carried over Europe by Syrian traders. Neither the Syrians nor the trade ceased when barbarian kingdoms replaced the Western Empire. After 476, Syrians still appear on the coasts of Belgium, France, Spain. Nor do they only appear as traders. There are Syrian popes. There will be a Syrian archbishop of Canterbury. Gold and silk are used in the barbarian courts. Spices and papyrus find their way to the monasteries of northern Europe. But about AD 700 all these cease. Gold disappears from European currency; eastern luxuries and Syrian merchants from barbarian Europe. A new European society presents itself before us. It is a society based on rural self-sufficiency: self-sufficiency which will afterwards find its expression in the forms of feudalism.

Pirenne suggested that the cause of this break in the eighth century was, in one word, Mahomet. By the time of his death in 632, the Prophet of Islam had already conquered Arabia, and his successors, immediately afterwards, set out to conquer the rest of the East. This Moslem conquest first of Syria and Egypt, then of North Africa and Spain, cut Europe off from the Mediterranean and thereby finally broke the lifeline by which, even after the fall of the Western Empire, the romanized society of Europe had been attached to the nutritive East. So Europe was turned in on itself, and society was gradually systematized on its new basis. It was systematized, again in one word, by Charlemagne: Charlemagne who, like Constantine, once again reorganized the coinage, abolishing the gold coins of the Empire, and establishing the system used in Britain until 1971—£ s d: the pound of twenty shillings, the shilling of twelve pence. From the time of Charlemagne, in the eighth century, for nearly 500 years, Europe outside Byzantium (and a few states in direct contact with the Arab world) had no regular gold coins. The old classical coin-names were taken over by the triumphant Moslems—the

drachma and the denarius became the dirhem and the dinar; and when Offa, the eighth-century king of Mercia, from his driblets of Welsh gold, minted a few gold coins, he put on them Arabic inscriptions. It was the only way to make them look real. In this and in other ways Charlemagne broke with the past: and the break was forced, essentially, by Mahomet. The Moslem conquest, says Pirenne, was 'the end of the classic tradition, the beginning of the Middle Ages ... without Mahomet, Charlemagne would have been inconceivable'.

Since 1937 Pirenne's famous thesis has provoked dozens of replies. There have been denials, modifications, questions. Today few historians accept it in his terms. But the problem which he stated remains, and so do the central facts which he saw. The old world had ended by the eighth century; a new world did then begin; and among the causes of the change we cannot exclude the Moslem invasions. However, we should remember that the Moslem invasions, though the most dramatic and the most permanent, were

73

44, 45 Portrait of Offa, King of Mercia 755–96, from a silver coin. Even his gold dinar (*right*) bears an Arabic inscription

not the only invasions of those years. There were also other invasions, some of them independent of the Moslem conquests, others involved with them. These were the invasions of the nomads. For the period between the fifth and the eighth centuries, between the political and the social end of the Roman Empire, is one of the great periods of nomadic irruptions. There were land-nomads and sea-nomads, both of whom suddenly, with their superior mobility, enveloped and overpowered the settled populations of the civilized world. Before we consider the Moslem conquests which absorbed and directed them, let us consider some of these nomads; and first let us consider the Eurasian land-nomads, the oldest problem of all.

For centuries the settled civilizations of the temperate zone—of the Mediterranean, of the Middle East, of India, of China—had had to defend themselves against the nomads of the wide steppe-lands which stretch from Siberia to northern Europe. These nomads were pastoral horsemen, relatively few in number, but fierce and mobile; and at times they formed themselves into great confederations which, either directly or indirectly—that is, either by appearing themselves or by driving other barbarians before them—threatened to overthrow the settled states of richer lands. Such was the confederation of the Hsiung-Nu, of about 200 BC, who put the Chinese Empire under tribute and pushed other invaders into Persia; such were the various

75

Charlemagne's impact upon the imagination of a later age is expressed in this stylized ary bust, made about 1350 to hold parts of his skull

46 A prosperous Vandal landowner leaving his North African
villa. (A mosaic of about 500 from Carthage)

Huns of the fourth and fifth centuries AD who invaded India and
terrorized the failing Roman Empire; and such, long afterwards,
were the Mongols, who in the thirteenth century would conquer
China and Persia and penetrate Europe as far as Poland and Hungary.
In the fourth century, one such commotion in the steppes sent the
Vandals into Europe: they would penetrate into Spain, leaving their
name in Andalusia, and in the next century would conquer North
Africa, Carthage and, from Carthage, Rome itself. In the sixth
century a similar commotion discharged into Europe another tribe
of invaders, the Avars. From their base in Hungary they in turn
drove other invaders into Italy and the Balkans. Under the impact of
these invasions all the work of Justinian crumbled. The Lombard
invasion of Italy finally ended the Roman system there. Slavs pushed
the Greeks and Illyrians into corners of the Balkan peninsula. And
the Avars themselves appeared repeatedly under the walls of Constantinople.

The Avars, like the Vandals, like all the steppe-nomads, were
horsemen. It was their horses, or rather their light, nimble ponies,

47 A barbarian horseman
(carved *c.* 700)

which gave these nomads their terrible mobility. They fought from
horseback, with bow and arrow, uncatchable, inescapable, un-
approachable. The Romans felt powerless before them: St Jerome,
who was in Bethlehem when they burst into the Middle East,
lamented the impotence of the Roman armies before men 'who
cannot walk on foot, and, once dismounted, count themselves dead'.
Only the Persians, who had always been most directly exposed to
them, had learned to deal effectively with such horsemen. They had
done so, well before the foundation of the Roman Empire, partly
by imitating their tactics—hence those 'Parthian shots' which the
Romans thought so ungentlemanly—but partly also by improving
on them. They had learned to breed strong horses, capable of carrying armed men, and of being armed themselves. These strong
Persian horses could not be copied by everyone: they needed special
feeding and were therefore expensive to maintain: mere subsistence
agriculture could not support them. But the Persians had shown the
way, and they themselves persevered in it. The revived Persian
Empire which fought against Rome and Byzantium for the 400

48, 49, 50 New animal engines of war. (*Left*) Armed war horse and 'cataphract': a Chinese figure from the Wei dynasty. Strong, weight-carrying horses had been bred by the Persians since before the foundation of the Roman Empire. They were used for hunting (*right*: Sassanian silver plate of Chosroes II) as well as in battle. (*Below right*) One-humped Arabian camels, in a medieval illumination. The introduction of the camel in the third century altered the whole defence problem of Roman and Byzantine Africa

years from AD 250 to 650 was a mounted aristocracy. The Persian peasants and towns paid dearly for defence by heavily armed noble horsemen, and the 'great horses' were sustained on the difference. Other societies, exposed to nomad attack, looked with envy on Persia. The 'Martial Emperor' of China, Han Wu-Ti, who for the 54 years of his reign (140 to 87 BC) sustained a fierce struggle with the nomadic Huns on his northern frontier, was filled with admiration and envy for 'the blood-sweating horses of Iran'—though he thought them too expensive to copy. Afterwards the emperors of Byzantium envied them too, and did copy them. The Byzantines called them, or rather their riders, cataphracts.

The agile steppe-pony of the nomads, the Persian 'great horse', the Byzantine cataphract: these were new engines which by the fifth and sixth centuries had changed the character of war. But there was also another new engine, no less important. If the horse-nomads threatened civilization on its northern flank, on its southern flank it was now equally threatened by a different type of nomad: the camel-nomads.

The camel, the one-humped Arabian camel, came late to Africa. The ancient Egyptians never knew it: it was only the Persian conquest which brought it to Egypt. Even when it reached Egypt it took a long time to move beyond it. The Carthaginians, in all the time of their empire, never knew it: it was the Roman conquest which brought it, long afterwards, to north-west Africa. In fact, it seems, it was the African emperor Septimius Severus who imported it, about AD 200, and it took more than a century before it was acclimatized. This deliberate introduction of the camel into North Africa was a fact of enormous importance. Until that time, North Africa, Roman Africa, was blocked to the South by steppe and desert. The introduction of the camel, says the French historian E.-F. Gautier, lifted the blockade: it was 'an economic revolution comparable—it is no exaggeration to say—with the introduction of the railway, the motor-car and the airplane'.

But if the introduction of the camel brought new benefits to Roman Africa, it also brought new, unexpected dangers. Up to that time the Romans had hardly needed to defend Africa to the south. All along the coast they had built up a wonderfully prosperous civilization: a civilization whose relics are still visible in splendid Roman cities like Volubilis, Lepcis Magna, or Timgad. Roman Africa was so rich and populous that it contained some 250 bishoprics, so prosperous and well-tilled that, according to an Arab historian, 'the whole country from Tripoli to Tangier was nothing but one shaded grove, one continuous series of villages'. This prosperity, admittedly, was achieved at a price. It was the prosperity of land-lords whose exploited, enslaved peasants took refuge in heresy and sometimes violence. But so long as the outer frontier was secure, inner peace could be kept. One outer frontier was already broken in the fifth century, when Rome lost control of the sea. Hence the Vandal invasion of Africa, which convulsed society till Justinian, by recovering sea-power, restored Roman rule. But then the other frontier was turned. When the possibilities of the camel had been exploited, not only by the provincials, for transport, but by nomads of the desert, for conquest, the whole problem of defence was altered. The desert, from being an empty waste, became, like the northern steppes, the source of sudden attack, fierce and swift. A century before the Arabs appeared, the camel-nomads of the desert had broken up the barely restored unity and prosperity of Roman Africa. That unity, that prosperity, would not be seen again until 1,300 years had passed and the French had occupied not only the coastal strip but the desert too.

Thus equally to the north and to the south of civilization, new enemies appeared. In the sixth century, Rome and Persia, Justinian and Chosroes continue their struggles—struggles which seem in retrospect a civil war of civilization—while the barbarians are at the gate. And in the seventh century the sudden revolution in Arabia acts as a catalyst, bringing all the enemies of civilization together with overwhelming force. The convulsion of the desert, the message of the Prophet, gave a new impact or a new coherence to these scattered nomadic tribes and launched them suddenly, and all at once, upon the two proud empires still locked in the traditional postures of conventional war.

The most dramatic episode in the miraculous series of Moslem conquests is perhaps the ruin of Persia. Never did the Persian monarchy seem so firm as in the early seventh century. In 612, in the course of their Byzantine wars, the Persian armies reached Antioch; in 614 they took Jerusalem and carried off the Cross of Christ; in 618 they were at Alexandria. It seemed as if the conquests of Cyrus and Cambyses were to be repeated. Then the tide turned. The Byzantine emperor Heraclius raised an army in Asia Minor and in a brilliant campaign recovered all, including the Cross, and took for

51 The emperor Heraclius holding the Holy Cross which he recaptured from the Persians in 629—only to lose it, within a few years, to the Arab invaders

ПЄРСН РѣВХТА ЦРНГРА

fub ifto coftantino venit p

52 Constantinople under Persian assault in 626. In the same year the imperial city, represented by the six towers and two archers at left, also survived an attack by the Avars

himself the title of *Basileus*, Great King, hitherto monopolized by
the King of Persia. Instead of the conquests of Cyrus and Cambyses,
it now seemed as if the conquests of Alexander were to be repeated.
That was in 630. Who would have guessed that within ten years both
these great empires would be prostrated: that the Byzantine Empire
would be utterly defeated, that Syria and Egypt would be lost for
ever, that Jerusalem and the Cross of Christ would again pass to the
infidel; and that the Persian Empire, the State which, with its great
horses and its armed chivalry, had seemingly invented the perfect
device against nomad invaders, would dissolve in a day? Yet this is
what happened. It happened because a new social force had arisen in
the Middle East: a force which combined the confederative powers
of an Attila or a Genghis Khan with the intoxication of a new
ideology: Islam.

Even so, we may ask, why did both Persia and Byzantium so
easily crumble before the attack? What weakness caused two such
ancient, famous, historic empires so suddenly to break up? When
we ask this question, we have to remember two facts. First, there is
heresy; secondly, there is the heavy cost of those 'great horses'.

First, heresy. The function of heresy in history is fascinating, but

82

53 The strife caused by the Arian heresy: these ninth-century miniatures show (*above*) a group of orthodox Christians, including a bishop, fleeing for their lives in a boat; and Arians setting fire to an orthodox church

it is never simple. We often think of heresy as being merely intellectual. Often it is intellectual. Always it is devised by intellectuals. But in its most powerful form it is often national, generally social, sometimes both. When a society is conquered, and apparently absorbed by its conquerors, it often retains its identity by insisting on a religious difference. The barbarians who were absorbed by Rome all adopted the heretical Arian, not the orthodox Athanasian form of Christianity—until Roman power had collapsed, after which they ceased to mind. When the Persians were conquered by the Arabs, they perversely adopted the heretical Shi'a, not the orthodox Sunni form of Islam. The Turkish Khazars, on the fringe of Persia, and the Turkish Uighurs, on the fringe of China, emphasized their independence by adopting, respectively, the Jewish and the Manichaean religions. Even today the Scots and the Irish show a deplorable indifference to the self-evident truths of the Anglican Church. In these instances heresy is the sign of national dissent. But it also symbolizes social dissent, which national differences sometimes merely sharpen. Almost all medieval heresies were the heresies of dissident social groups protesting against a society in which they felt themselves to be misfits. And so, in the early centuries of the Church, throughout the Middle East and Africa, there were national and social tensions disguised as heresy. Syrians, Egyptians, Berbers had not accepted the pagan orthodoxy imposed by Roman emperors and the privileged classes in Greco-Roman towns. Nor would they afterwards accept the Christian orthodoxy imposed by the same authorities. In Africa the Berbers of the fourth and fifth centuries supported the separatist, puritan 'Donatist' movement. St Augustine thundered away at them and in the end the Donatist Church ceased to exist. But the discontent did not, and the Vandal invaders were able to exploit it. In the East there was similar opposition. Syrians and Egyptians presumed to describe the orthodoxy of Constantinople as 'royalism'—a mere religion of state. Justinian persecuted these impertinent heretics of the outer empire. Consequently, in the outer empire, the invading Arabs, when they came, would be seen as deliverers both of heretics from an intolerant Church and of Orientals from foreign, Greek rule.

The same was true of Persia. There the established religion was the official Zoroastrianism of the state and its equestrian aristocracy. But that state and that aristocracy were expensive to maintain, and the townsmen and peasants of Persia were crushed to pay for the chivalry which kept the northern nomads at bay. They too turned to heresy: to Zoroastrian heresies, of which there were many. The result was the same as in the Byzantine Empire. In the hour of national crisis the heretics did not support the religion of state, and when the fatal blow was struck the great horsemen of Iran crumbled before it through lack of support at home. The social isolation of their class is shown by the complete destruction of their orthodoxy. The religion of Persia, the authentic, native, national religion of Zoroaster, the religion of Darius and Xerxes which the Sassanian kings had revived, had become the religion of a class. When that class was defeated, the religion disappeared: having no roots in the people, it withered away. Exactly the same thing would happen 800 years later when the feudal chivalry of Hungary would collapse before the Turks and the long-exploited 'heretical' Greek peasants would welcome the Moslem conquerors against their Catholic Venetian and Genoese overlords.

So the Persian great horses and the Byzantine cataphracts crumbled before the Arab attack, and the Arabs, having quickly digested their huge conquests, pressed on to extend them. Constantinople indeed they could not take. They were driven back from it by the new device of Greek fire—an opportune Syrian invention of explosive flames shot from copper tubes. But that check only diverted their force; it did not break it. They turned from the North to the South, mobilized the nomads of the African desert, swept along the Berber coast, and rolled up the weakened Byzantine positions. In 711 they crossed the Straits of Gibraltar and destroyed the Visigothic kingdom of Spain. Six years later, at the other end of the Mediterranean, they crossed the Hellespont and again appeared before Constantinople, which they besieged by land and sea. The Mediterranean, from end to end, had become their lake.

The early years of the eighth century—the years when the invasions of the Avars and the Lombards had been followed by the

54 'Greek fire' was the Byzantine navy's secret weapon in their battles with the Arabs after *c*. 67

mixture of petroleum, sulphur, and pitch, it is shown in action in this illumination of *c.* 1300

conquests of the Arabs, were indeed the darkest age of Europe. Outside the mutilated empire of Byzantium, European civilization had by then shrunk to its smallest cell. It was the cell created by St Benedict in the days of Theodoric, the Gothic king of Italy: the monastic cell, with its self-contained economy, capable of survival in the oddest places and in the worst times, like a seed in the winter *detritus* of Nature. For this was the essential character of Benedictine monasticism. Every cell was independent. If one perished, others survived. If all but one perished, the system could yet be re-created from one survivor. And in fact, in those terrible years, all the most famous of the early monasteries would be destroyed, beginning with St Benedict's own monastery, Monte Cassino, whose destruction by the Lombards took place in 581. The monastery of Luxeuil, planted in Burgundy by the Irish missionary St Columban, would be destroyed later by the Saracens. No one could predict what might be the safest place, where the seed could safely lie. By the year 700 European learning had fled to the bogs of Ireland or the wild coast of Northumbria. It was in the monasteries of Ireland that fugitive scholars preserved a knowledge of the Latin and even of the Greek

55 St Benedict of Nursia, founder of the monastery of Monte Cassino. (A late ninth-century fresco)

56 Page from a Carolingian codex produced in the abbey of St Gall, Switzerland; an early copy of the Rule of St Benedict

classics. It was in a monastery in Northumbria that the greatest scholar of his time, the greatest historian of the whole Middle Ages, the Venerable Bede, lived and wrote. And it was from the monasteries of Ireland and England, in the eighth and ninth centuries, that English and Irish fugitives would return to a devastated Europe: men like the Englishmen St Boniface, who would convert the Germans to Christianity, Alcuin of York, the teacher of Charlemagne, or the Irishman John Scotus Erigena, who went to teach at the court of the Emperor Charles the Bald. Some of these fugitives had fled from England and Ireland before the advance of yet another race of mobile nomads who were now descending on the helpless relics of the Western Empire: the Viking sea-nomads who, from the end of the eighth century, came every year to burn and loot the monasteries on the seashore or up the rivers accessible to their long boats. Among the first to be sacked were the beacons of the Celtic and Northumbrian Church: Iona, St Columba's abbey, the capital of the Celtic Church in Scotland; Lindisfarne, its daughter-house on Holy Island in Northumberland, the first foothold of the Celtic Church in England; and Jarrow itself, the monastery of the Venerable Bede.

57 An islet in Lough Erne is the site of this sixth-century Celtic monastery, one of the remote havens of refuge from the barbarians

What were these Vikings doing? What sudden force drove these piratical Northmen to range over the seas and rivers of Europe, creating havoc? It used to be supposed that it was merely a sudden, unexplained growth of population in Scandinavia which lay behind this extraordinary outburst. No doubt this is true: so vast an expansion cannot have been sustained by a static population. But the scope and direction of the raids point also to other motives. There were opportunities abroad as well as pressures at home; and these opportunities link together the Viking raids and the Moslem conquests.

For the Moslem conquests were not confined to the provinces of the Persian and Byzantine empires: they were also carried to Central Asia and Africa; and in Central Asia and Africa new sources of wealth were opened up. In Khorasan, to the east of Persia, and in Transoxiana beyond it, between Kashmir and the Aral Sea, vast mines of silver were discovered. The scenes which an Arab writer describes at the silver mine of Banjahîr in Afghanistan are likened by a modern historian to the gold-rush at Klondike. Afterwards, the Arabs conquered Nubia, the Sudan, with its famous gold mines. They also rifled the tombs of the Pharaohs in Egypt, churches and temples in the Byzantine and Persian east. Thanks to these fabulous supplies first of silver, then of gold, they were able to purchase what they wanted from the barbarian kingdoms of Europe; and what they wanted, and what the barbarian kingdoms in their ruined state could supply, were not, of course, luxuries or manufactures—never, even while the Western Empire had lasted, had they produced those—but the simplest of raw materials: furs, weapons, timber, and above all their own bodies: eunuchs and slaves.

It was one of the functions of the Vikings to supply these goods. Half traders, half pirates, they ranged over all northern Europe, and in their ranging, or through the method of piracy, they collected furs and kidnapped human beings. For preference they dealt in heathen Slavs, since Christian States had less compunction in handling a slave-trade in heathen bodies—they could always quote that useful text, *Leviticus* xxv, 44. So the Vikings fed both Byzantium and the rich new civilization of Islam with the goods which

58, 59 Viking relics: a carved head used as a cart-ornament, and a ship's prow, both from the same ninth-century grave in Oseberg

they demanded and for which they could pay. In so doing they penetrated all the coasts and rivers of Europe. They set up principalities in Russia, England, France; they supplied a Nordic 'Varangian' guard to the Emperors of Constantinople; they served as mercenary soldiers to the Khan of the Jewish Khazars on the lower Volga; and their infamous traffic, passing indirectly through western Europe as well as directly through the Volga and the

Caspian Sea, provided some of the wealth which would create pockets of light in the Dark Ages. It was their traffic which would bring *aurum arabicum*, Arabic gold—*aurum infelix*, unhappy gold, as humane men preferred to call it, for it was the price of humanity—to the court of Charlemagne; and it was the same Arabic (or Byzantine) gold with which, in the tenth century, the Viking princes of the great slaving city of Kiev would mint their first golden coins.

For if the Vikings were the pioneers, the princes of Europe, or some of them, were the middlemen of the new slave-trade. They licensed it and profited by it, though they left the direct traffic in it to Jews, who could move most easily across the frontiers of the two societies. We have plenty of evidence of this trade and its routes—down the Volga towards Persia, down the Danube towards Constantinople, down the Rhône to Narbonne and into Moslem Spain. Liutprand of Cremona, the ambassador of the West who, in the tenth century, stood agog before the kaleidoscopic pageantry of the Byzantine court, tells us that it was the merchants of Verdun who, for the immense profit of the trade, made boys into eunuchs and sold them through Moorish Spain to the rich Moslem world: 'the last abomination', exclaims Gibbon, 'of the abominable slave trade'. The trade has left its mark in the languages of both Christendom and Islam. *Sclavi*, 'Slavs', has formed, in every European language, the word for slaves; and the same word, *Sakáliba*, has provided the Arabic word for eunuchs.

Such were the dark ages of Europe, the golden age of Islam. Do they not remind us of another period, when the boot was on the other leg? In the sixteenth century vast new supplies of precious metals, this time discovered in the Far West, would create a golden age for Europe. In order to work the machine which sustained that high culture, the Europeans, in their turn, needed slaves and they too bought them where they could. Exploiting the internal wars of black Africa, and the greed of native kings, their agents stuffed their ships with kidnapped human cattle, and the traffic was justified, as long as such justification was thought necessary, and would serve, by the argument that negroes were heathen—or, if Christian, were anyway the children of Ham, or Canaan, destined by their father's

60 St Adalbert of Prague, martyred by the heathen Prussians in 997, intercedes with Boleslav I, prince of Poland, for the release of three of his subjects from a Jewish slave-trader. (A twelfth-century relief from Gniezno Cathedral)

curse to perpetual servitude. (There was always that useful text, *Genesis* IX, 25.) The slave-kidnappers and slave-traders who fed the sugar-mills of Brazil and the plantations of North America in the seventeenth and eighteenth centuries were the Christian equivalent of the Vikings and Jews who had fed the Moslem lands in the eighth, ninth and tenth centuries. They did not, it is true, make them eunuchs; but some of the punishments they inflicted were hardly better.

Yet, out of this dark age, Europe revived. It revived because it discovered and developed a new form of social organization; a form which provided the means of survival, resistance and ultimately aggression against its oppressors and exploiters. That form was feudalism; and it was devised, it seems, in the very darkest years of the dark century: the years when Constantinople in the East and France in the West were facing the apparently invincible advance of the Arab conquerors.

It was throughout the winter of 717–18 that the Arabs laid their second and greatest siege to Constantinople. Once again they were

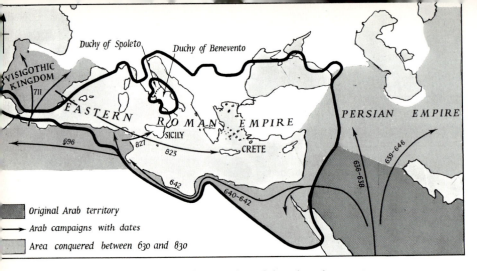

Duchy of Spoleto Duchy of Benevento

VISIGOTHIC
KINGDOM
711

EASTERN ROMAN EMPIRE

PERSIAN EMPIRE

SICILY

696   827
             823   CRETE

642
          640-642

636-638

639-646

Original Arab territory

Arab campaigns with dates

Area conquered between 630 and 830

61 Arab conquests in the seventh, eighth and ninth centuries

ultimately driven off; but before long they would return, year after year, to attack the empire. In the course of these struggles, and in order to sustain them, the Byzantine emperors reorganized the whole basis of the empire. Having already adopted the Persian system of armed horsemen, cataphracts, they now went further and adopted the Persian system of uniting military and civil power. By degrees, under each new military threat, the empire became a military system sustained by hereditary landlords: in other words, by a kind of feudalism. And meanwhile, in the West, the same pressure was leading to the same results. In 720, only two years after the great siege of Constantinople, the Arabs, having conquered Spain, crossed the Pyrenees. They took Narbonne, and sacked the greatest monasteries of southern France. Then they continued their northward march as far as Poitiers. They had, says Gibbon, prolonged their victorious line of march more than 1,000 miles from Gibraltar to the banks of the Loire:

'The repetition of an equal space would have carried the Saracens to the confines of Poland and the highlands of Scotland; the Rhine is not more impassable than the Nile or Euphrates, and the Arabian fleet might have sailed without a naval combat into the mouth of the Thames. Perhaps the interpretation of the Koran would now be taught in the schools of Oxford, and her pulpits might demonstrate to a circumcised people the sanctity and truth of the revelation of Mohammed.'

'From such calamities', says Gibbon, 'was Christendom delivered by the genius and fortune of one man.' That one man was, of course, Charles Martel, the 'mayor of the palace' and effective ruler of the Frankish kingdom who, in the battle of Poitiers, defeated the Arabs at this, the farthest point of their advance. It was a historic moment, no less dramatic, though perhaps less important, than the lifting of the siege of Constantinople; and Gibbon loses none of his art in relating it:

'It might have been expected that the saviour of Christendom would have been canonized, or at least applauded, by the gratitude of the clergy, who are indebted to his sword for their present existence. But in the public distress the mayor of the palace had been compelled to apply the riches, or at least the revenues, of the bishops and abbots to the relief of the state and the reward of the soldiers. His merits were forgotten, his sacrilege alone remembered, and in an epistle to a Carlovingian prince, a Gallic synod presumes to declare that his ancestor was damned; that on the opening of his tomb the spectators were affrighted by a smell of fire and the aspect of a horrid dragon; and that a saint of the time was indulged with a pleasant vision of the soul and body of Charles Martel burning, to all eternity, in the abyss of hell.'

Modern historians quibble at some details of Gibbon's account. The battle of Poitiers, they say, was of small significance, and the Arabs were defeated by logistics rather than by Charles Martel. But I have given it partly (I admit) because it is so enjoyable and partly because it draws attention to two important facts. Charles Martel, the grandfather of Charlemagne, succeeded in halting the Moslem invasion of western Europe; but he did so, and his successors continued the process, at the expense of a massive secularization of Church property. These two facts are intimately connected. They are connected by a third fact which Gibbon does not mention. The purpose of the immediate secularization, the cause of the ultimate success, was a new institution, which was to turn Christendom from a defeated and demoralized into a conquering power. Charles Martel, like the emperors of Byzantium, recognized that if these terrible mobile invaders were to be held, there was no alternative to the Persian system. There must be 'great horses', cataphracts. These 'great horses', expensive though they were, must be maintained. In order to maintain them, the Persians had depressed their towns and peasants, and the result had been that the cataphracts had been isolated and had gone down alone. Western European cataphracts would be no less expensive. But they were essential. In order to find the economic surplus on which to maintain them, Charles Martel endowed his new horsed warriors, his knights, with lands confiscated from the Church. As at the Reformation, as in the century of the Enlightenment—successive stages in the later progress of mankind—the first recovery of Europe from its darkest age was secured by the salutary reduction of an over-endowed Church.

Charles Martel, by endowing a new class of expensively armed knights, mounted on expensively maintained 'great horses', can be called the founder of European feudalism: that elaborate system of military tenures and military obligations which is the hallmark of the European middle ages. Today we often use the word 'feudalism' in a loose sense, to imply a hierarchical system based on land. We speak of feudal manners when we merely mean privilege of landlords, and of a feudal reaction when we merely mean a recovery of predominance by the landed interest. But European feudalism meant something far clearer than this. It meant an exact relationship between the tenure of land and military duty; and that duty was the duty of 'knight-service'. The landlord had to serve as a knight, or to put into the field so many knights, and the knight had to bring his tenants into the field with him. The central element in the whole system was the knight. Around him grew up an entire system of society: a system of economy, a system of morals, a system of values; but he was the essential figure of it all. And this central figure, this knight, the answer to Europe's problem, without whom we can hardly conceive of medieval society or appreciate its unique character, was no other than a western adaptation of that same Persian horseman who had been the model also of the Byzantine cataphract. Well may an American historian, Mr William McNeill, write, in his excellent book *The Rise of the West*, that Iran—Persia— was the model for Europe.

Moreover, the European knight maintained by Charles Martel and his successors had one great advantage over his Persian or Byzantine model. He had the advantage of a little device which seems obvious to us—we have used it ever since—but which was entirely unknown to Antiquity and which seems to have been unknown until the time of Charles Martel. This little device, whose history has recently been set out with great clarity by Mr Lynn White, was that simple but essential aid to every horseman, the stirrup. I say that the stirrup 'seems to have been unknown' before Charles Martel because, in fact, there is great controversy about the date of its invention. Michael Rostovtzeff, the greatest of modern historians of Rome, believed that he had discovered the use of stirrups among the Sarmatians, the half-Persian horsed bowmen of the South Russian steppe; and thence it has been presumed that the Sarmatian Alans and their pupils the German Vandals also had stirrups. But now this is doubted, and although certainty is hard to

62, 63 The introduction of the stirrup increased the European knight's effectiveness. (*Left*) A silver-plated medieval stirrup from Lithuania; (*right*) relief of an armed knight from Limoges

attain—archaeologists have good reason to curse St Boniface for converting the Germans to Christianity before their pagan burials had shown whether they used stirrups or not—it seems that stirrups were introduced to the West in the days of Charles Martel. At all events, it seems clear that he was the first to exploit the invention, and consequently his west European knights had a force which had been enjoyed by neither Persian horsemen nor Byzantine cataphracts. Thanks to his stirrups, the Frankish knight could wield his weapon with far greater force and certainty. He did not need, perhaps he disdained, to use the bow. He was not restricted to light movements with the lance. Having a firm seat, he could fight without restraint. He could slash with his sword without becoming unhorsed by an air-shot, and he could place his lance in the rest and charge with the whole weight of horse and man behind it, unafraid of being himself airborne by the impact. Thus the stirrup, as adapted in Europe, made the knight a new and more effective engine of war, and the knight, as encased in the new economic system, made feudalism a new and—for its time—more effective system of society.

I have described the western monastery, that self-contained economic unit of corn wine, and oil, animated by the spirit of St Benedict, as the simple cell which could survive and carry the seeds of western life even through the grim winter of the Dark Ages. Similarly, feudalism—the military unit of armoured horse, armoured knight and stirrups—could be described as the simple cell which could preserve, concentrate and release the residual powers of European society, almost totally annihilated in the days of the Moslem and Viking conquests. Ultimately, both monasticism and feudalism would have a lurid, varied history. The simple cell of St Benedict would be transformed into the great agricultural factories of the Cistercians, the magnificent abbeys of the thirteenth century, the lordly parasites of the late Middle Ages. The simple cell of feudalism would develop into a system, a way of life, which behind a façade of elaborate chivalry would create, instead of unity, discipline and strength, a European anarchy. But those times, those developments, were not to be foreseen in the eighth century. Then the two forces were both in embryo; an embryo hardly to be

64 Gregory the Great, from an early eleventh-
century edition of his *Commentary on Ezekiel*

noticed, among the rottenness of surrounding society, by the
triumphant barbarians, or the Moslems enjoying their golden age.

Moreover, in those years of ferment and change, these two cells,
the monastic cell and the feudal cell, were increasingly drawn
together. One of the contrasts made by Pirenne between Europe
before and after the Moslem conquests is the contrast between a
secular and a clerical society. The society of western Europe before
Charlemagne had been essentially secular. In the Roman Empire
Christianity had owed its establishment to Constantine, to the
state. Therefore the Church had been subordinate to the state, the
clergy to the laity. The dissolution of the Western Empire had not
altered that. The pope might have gained power in Rome, but he
remained subject to the emperor in the East. Even the greatest of
popes, Gregory the Great, expressed only flattery, devotion, sub-
mission, to even the worst of emperors, 'the abominable Phocas'
who had pushed his way, by murder, to the throne. 'As a subject
and a Christian', says Gibbon, 'it was the duty of Gregory to
acquiesce in the established government; but the joyful applause
with which he salutes the fortune of the assassin has sullied with

indelible disgrace the character of the saint.' And in the barbarian kingdoms the pattern is the same: 'the political power of the kings' remarks Pirenne, 'like that of the emperors, was purely secular'. No religious ceremony was celebrated on their accession. They did not reign by the grace of God. 'None of their court functionaries were ecclesiastics. All their ministers and officials were laymen'—laymen with a lay attitude, trained in lay letters, the residue of the classic past. The bishops were appointed by the kings and obedient to them, even if the kings themselves were heretics.

But such a lay society, feeble as it was, did not outlast the period of the Moslem invasions. It had no vital cell of its own to survive the winter season, and it shrivelled up. When the family of Charles Martel sought to re-create western life, it was not on that old secular basis that they sought to do it. A new impulse was needed; and that new impulse had to be religious. Monasticism, puritanism, rigid doctrine—these were the forces which alone, it seemed, could re-inspire the West, provide the spiritual or intellectual or ideological force to animate the new 'feudal' resistance. So Charles Martel, though he secularized Church property, had no intention of undermining the Church. On the contrary, he summoned monks from England and Ireland to reorganize the Frankish Church, and his grandson Charlemagne and his great-grandson Louis the Pious used the great monasteries they founded—'the cultural centres of the Carolingian empire', as they have been called—as a source of power for a new policy: a policy of alliance with the pope, support of the pope, emancipation of the pope from the still secular Eastern Empire and, ultimately, puritan reform of the papacy. By these methods they would unite the two new cells of religious and feudal power. They would unite them at all levels: not only at the top, in politics, but all through society—for Christianity still possessed its proselytizing spirit, its vitalizing social power: there was no danger, as yet, that the Christian knights, like the Persian horsemen, would go down alone. Out of this union, this intimate social and political union of ideological and military force, would come, in due time, the combined spiritual and material counter-attack of the enslaved West against its Moslem exploiters: the Crusades.

IV THE CRUSADES

The Crusades, that extraordinary series of holy wars, that long struggle in the Levant between East and West, Christendom and Islam, which began so theatrically in the eleventh century and petered out so ignominiously in the thirteenth, were described by Gibbon as 'the World's Debate'. The world has debated about them a good deal since and will no doubt go on debating. I intend to debate about them now.

At first, the view was clear enough. The simple crusaders, who paused to chronicle their violent but holy deeds, and ended each chapter of carnage with devout scriptural ejaculations, questioned their own motives no more than the Spanish conquistadors of the sixteenth century. To them, the Turks were the infamous, accursed unbelievers, 'God's enemies and ours', while the Christians who perished in battle went up to Heaven to be robed in white and receive the palm of martyrdom. After the Reformation, some Protestants ventured to express doubt. The only gainer by all this great adventure, wrote Thomas Fuller in the reign of Charles I, was the pope; 'all other princes of Europe, if they cast up their audit, shall find themselves losers'; the Crusades, he argued, were both the fruit and the cause of superstition; the pope, for his profit, 'made all Jerusalem *Golgotha*, a place for skulls, and all the Holy Land *Aceldama*, a field of blood'. But good Catholics were not dismayed. At the court of Louis XIV, if the Abbé Fleury walked warily, his rival, the fashionable Jesuit Louis Maimbourg, brandished his pen boldly. To him the Crusades were still holy wars, whose every barbarity was justified by their high spiritual aim; and he described with relish how the Christians, once in possession of Jerusalem, 'used to their full extent the rights of victory . . . . Everywhere one could see nothing but heads flying, legs hacked off, arms cut down, bodies in slices . . . they killed the very children in their mothers' arms to exterminate, if possible, that accursed race, as God formerly wished should be done to the Amalekites.'

Then, in the mid-eighteenth century, came a change. It was the time when religious controversy was giving way to 'philosophy'. All the great 'philosophical historians' of the Enlightenment turned their minds to the problem of the Crusades. The more incomprehensible it seemed to those cool, rational spirits, the more they felt the necessity of comprehending it. What had hitherto seemed perfectly right and natural did not seem right at all to them. The example of Saul and the Amalekites provided them with neither explanation nor justification. But they were not content to denounce or even to doubt. Believing that all men are fundamentally similar, and their actions ultimately explicable, they sought for psychological or social keys, and to find those keys they asked secular questions. What force could have launched this strange series of migrations in which, in the words of the astonished Byzantine princess who had witnessed it, Europe was loosened from its foundations and hurled against Asia? What was the real historical significance of those incredible adventures? What were the ultimate consequences for Europe and for Asia?

In their answers to these questions, the eighteenth-century historians sometimes differed in detail or in emphasis, but in general they agreed. On a superficial view, unquestionably, the Crusades were a deplorable outburst of fanaticism and folly. They were contrary to justice and common sense. With what justice, asked Voltaire, could the barbarian princes of Europe claim for themselves provinces which had been seized by the Turks not from them but from the Emperor of the East? By what rule of sense, asked Gibbon, did those descendants of German, Frankish and Norman conquerors assume that time had consecrated their own acquisitions in Europe but not those of the Moslems in Asia? If the eighteenth-century historians allowed any credit to Christian princes, it was not for enthusiasm but for scepticism in the holy cause. The only virtue of our William Rufus, said Hume, was his intelligent immunity from that epidemical folly. The only fault of St Louis, King of France, said Voltaire, was his liability to it. Voltaire's heroes were

65 A crusader doing homage: thirteenth-century illumination from an English

the Emperor Frederick II, who negotiated instead of fighting with the Sultan and found himself the victim of a papal crusade as a result, and the great enemy of the crusaders, Saladin, who having beaten the Christians in battle, bequeathed his wealth impartially to the Moslem, Jewish and Christian poor.

But causes are distinct from consequences. If the cause of the Crusades was human fanaticism, what was the result? It was not, certainly, the permanent establishment of Christian kingdoms in the East. The Christian kingdom of Jerusalem continued for less than a century. The Christian virtues, such as they were, evaporated in the East. The Christian dynasties ran out. The fathers might slaughter the Jews of Germany and the infidels of Palestine, catapult the heads of their prisoners into besieged cities, and wade through holy massacres singing *Te Deums* with tears of joy; but the sons—or rather the successors, for there was a dearth of sons—settled down to a life of luxurious co-existence in which feudal bonds were rotted and oriental tastes indulged. By the end of the thirteenth century all was over. The adventure was finished.

And what, if any, had been the profit of it? Voltaire wrote that Asia Minor was a gulf in which Europe was swallowed up, the tomb of over two million Europeans. Its only gift to Europe, he said, was leprosy. Gibbon added silk, sugar and windmills (but it seems that he may have been wrong about the windmills). If Europe gained anything, both agreed, it was very indirectly. The crusading nobles dissipated their estates and extinguished their families in those costly expeditions. But this dissipation and this extinction led to unexpected advantages for society. In order to equip themselves, the nobles were obliged to sell charters of freedom 'which unlocked the fetters of the slave, secured the farm of the peasant and the shop of the artificer, and gradually restored a substance and a soul to the most numerous and useful part of the community. The conflagration which destroyed the tall and barren trees of the forest gave air and scope to the vegetation of the smaller and nutritive plants of the soil.'

Some of the eighteenth-century historians allowed more direct advantages. William Robertson, the great Scottish historian, who was a minister of the Presbyterian Kirk and Moderator of its General

Assembly, allowed that the Crusades were 'a singular monument of human folly', but he saw them also as 'the first event that roused Europe from the lethargy in which it had long been sunk', and he ascribed to them certain 'beneficial consequences which had neither been foreseen nor expected'. The Italian cities, which conveyed, financed and exploited the Crusades, grew in wealth and created the lay culture of Europe; even the crusaders themselves were improved by contact with Moslem civility; and so, ultimately, 'to these wild expeditions, the effect of superstition or folly, we owe the first gleams of light which tended to dispel barbarism and ignorance'. But even here Gibbon dissented. 'Great', he admitted, 'was the increase and rapid the progress, during the 200 years of the Crusades, and some philosophers have applauded the propitious influence of those holy wars, which appear to me to have checked rather than forwarded the maturity of Europe. The lives and labours of millions which were buried in the East would have been more profitably employed in the improvement of their native country; the accumulated stock of industry and wealth would have overflowed in navigation and trade; and the Latins would have been enriched . . . by a pure and friendly correspondence with the climates of the East.'

So the historians of the eighteenth century debated. Since then, the material for debate has vastly grown. We know, or can know, far more than they did about the politics and the property transactions and the theological discussions of the Crusades. But these additional details, though they may add depth and complexity to historical problems, do not of themselves solve them; to think that they do is a common mistake of scholars. The great problems remain the same. What was the cause and function of the Crusades? Did they advance or retard the progress of Europe, and if so, how? Why did they occur when they did? Why did they break out in the eleventh century? And why did they end in the thirteenth? For although Crusades continued to be preached, and even occasionally launched, after the middle of the thirteenth century, the taste for them had gone by then. When the warriors of the Fourth Crusade had turned aside from the Moslem East to sack the Christian city of Constantinople, and popes were preaching crusades not against the infidel, or to recover the holy places from the Turks, but against Christian kings and Christian preachers who had the misfortune to differ from them on points of jurisdiction or theology, it was difficult to rouse that popular enthusiasm which had once caused clergy and laity alike to respond to Pope Urban II's preaching of the First Crusade at Clermont and had drawn thousands after the barefoot Peter the Hermit, as he rode on his donkey through France and Germany, calling for volunteers. By the second half of the thirteenth century the idea of the Crusade might linger on, for popes to abuse, but its captivating power was extinct.

Four Crusades, then, filled the period in which we are interested: that is, four spectacular, full-scale expeditions punctuating a constant if less conspicuous movement to the East. I shall not try to describe them. Like Gibbon, I shall 'abridge the tedious and uniform narrative of their blind achievements, which were performed by strength and are described by ignorance'. I shall be content with a bald summary of the facts before going on to consider the less dramatic but more interesting problem of their general historical significance.

The first and most spectacular Crusade was preached in 1095. Its great scenes are familiar to all. They include the appeal of the emperor Alexius, the response of Pope Urban, the preaching of Peter the Hermit, the mustering of forces, the preliminary slaughter of the Jews in the cities of the Rhine and the Danube, the annihilation of the 'People's Crusade' in Hungary, and the ultimate convergence at Constantinople of the three Frankish armies which then set out across Asia Minor on the great, novel adventure, the first of western Europe's armed invasions of the East.

Since it was the first, how strange, almost miraculous, it must have seemed! We catch the sense of wonder and excitement in the early chronicles: a mixture of exaltation, credulity and cruelty which has no parallel till the equally barbarous invasion of the New World four centuries later. The emperor of Constantinople was understandably alarmed by the response to his appeal. He felt like the sorcerer's apprentice who had conjured up a force more terrible than he had imagined. But he contrived to exact oaths of fealty from the formidable Norman and Frankish princes, and then, with relief, to see them and their disorderly, rapacious armies off across the Bosphorus. Once in Asia, the crusaders found everything easier than they had expected. The 'infidels' were not united against them. There were religious differences, local rivalries to exploit. Nicaea, the gateway to the Seljuk Empire, fell to them. Then, after defeating the Turkish army at Dorylaeum, they pushed south, captured Antioch, and at last, after many adventures and many dissensions, took Jerusalem itself. By 1100 there was a Christian king of Jerusalem; there were also Christian princes ruling over Antioch, Tripolis and Edessa.

To capture kingdoms is one thing, to keep them is another. A generation later, the Christians in the East were more divided and the infidels more united. In 1144 Edessa, the principality of the Norman family of Courtenay, fell to the Turks.

66, 67 (*Left*) The emperor Alexius Comnenus, whose appeal for help against the Turks led to the First Crusade in 1095 (portrait on a contemporary electrum coin). In the subsequent campaign the siege of Antioch (*right*) was followed by the capture of Jerusalem

At once the alarm was raised. Was all the heroism of the conquerors to prove useless? The pope, the kings of Christendom were roused. The Second Crusade, designed to shore up the tottering Eastern principalities, was first preached by St Bernard at Vézelay in 1145, and was followed, as usual, by the massacre of the Jews in Germany; after which a splendid army, led by the kings of France and Germany, arrived in Constantinople. After that, all was disaster. Having lost their armies at Iconium and Damascus, the two kings returned separately and singly to Europe; and St Bernard, blamed as the cause of the disaster, excused himself by an ingenious reference to Moses, who had also promised, in the name of God, to lead the faithful into the Holy Land, only to see the first generation perish in the wilderness.

That meant that the next generation should have succeeded. In fact, it did not. The Third Crusade, the Crusade of 1188, was led by three of the most striking kings of medieval Europe: the almost legendary Frederick Barbarossa, most famous of medieval em-

68, 69 The Second Crusade was first preached in 1145 by St Bernard of Clairvaux, shown in the detail from a fifteenth-century painting by Jean Fouquet. (*Right*) The crusading armies of Louis VII and Conrad III arriving in Constantinople

perors; Philip Augustus, the unromantic, one-eyed, astute maker of the French monarchy; and Richard I, Coeur de Lion, the romantic, handsome, unastute King of England. They set out to recover Jerusalem itself, captured Acre, and found themselves faced by yet another romantic, chivalrous figure who has caught the imagination of the world, the Kurdish sultan of Egypt and Syria, Saladin. The Crusade ended in general recrimination. The emperor was drowned in a river in Armenia; the King of France returned home in order to dish his ally, the King of England, in Europe; and the King of England was left alternately admiring and imitating the prowess of his Moslem adversary, who remained firmly in command of Jerusalem.

When the crusaders next set out, it was no longer against the Turks. The Fourth Crusade of 1204 is indeed one of the most disreputable episodes in the history of chivalry. It was directed against Egypt—now, under the sultanate of Saladin, the real key of Moslem power in the Levant. But the Venetian merchant aristocracy who provided it with transport had other ideas. From the very first, the

70, 71, 72 Three striking figures led the Third Crusade of 1188: (*left*) the emperor Frederick Barbarossa; (*centre*) Philip Augustus, king of France; (*right*) Richard Coeur de Lion, King of England

rude warriors of Europe had looked with envy and distrust on the splendid imperial capital of Constantinople and 'that wicked Emperor' (as the first Norman chronicler always calls him) who had his doubts alike about their policy, their manners, and their theology. By the time three Crusades had passed, they were already thinking that the schismatical Greeks were no less wicked than the infidel Turks and that their city—that marvellous, imperial city filled with the treasures and tribute of centuries—was far richer and more desirable than the holy but seedy hill-town of Jerusalem.

So, this time, the Venetian senators easily persuaded the crusaders to adjust their course. They sailed not to Egypt but to Constantinople. In due course a fortunate opportunity arose. There was a dynastic crisis in the Byzantine Empire. The invaders took sides in it, and soon found themselves in a powerful posture. The rest followed easily. The appropriate passions of orthodoxy and cupidity were enflamed; and amid scenes which put the massacres of Antioch and Jerusalem in the shade, the crusaders, having entered it as allies, seized and sacked the greatest city of Europe. That was the turning-point in the history of Byzantium, the greatest blow ever suffered by the imperial city. Hitherto it had been thought impregnable; and indeed it had been impregnable. Like Troy, it had outlasted every attack from without. The Persians, the Avars, the Arabs had invested it in vain. But now a treacherous party, introduced as a supposed ally, gave it over, and it fell.

So, to compensate for the lost Frankish kingdom of Jerusalem, a new Frankish Empire of Constantinople was set up. It was not so large an empire as the old Greek Empire, because the fortunate prince, Baldwin count of Flanders, having won the lottery, had to pay off his allies and bankers. So the outer provinces of the empire were partitioned among the other crusading princes; the greatest harbours and most valuable islands were quietly annexed by the prudent Venetians; and even Constantinople itself did not pass intact to its new ruler. The treasures which Constantine had gathered into his city from all quarters of the Roman Empire—from Delphi, from Rome, from Ephesus, from Egypt—were scattered again, destroyed in the pillage, or carried off, like the great bronze horses

73 (*Above*) Saladin, the Kurdish sultan of Egypt and Syria, being unhorsed by Richard Coeur de Lion: an unflattering picture from the Luttrell Psalter, *c.* 1340

74 Crusaders at Constantinople: an illustration from Archbishop William of Tyre's *History of Deeds Done beyond the Sea*

of Lysippus, to decorate the triumphant capitalist city, the real profiteer of the Crusades, Venice.

Such, in briefest outline, is the history of the first four Crusades. I will say no more about their course. What I wish to do is to place them, if I can, in some historical context and perspective: that is, first to set the whole movement against the secular background of the time, and secondly to see it in relation to other episodes in the expansion of Europe. For the historians of the Crusades have too often treated them in isolation. In fact, I believe, they should be seen as part of a larger social process which was characteristic of these two centuries. Moreover, behind their medieval, archaic, theological romantic colouring, the Crusades—I suggest—are remarkably similar to certain other stages in the expansion of Europe which, since they occurred in later times, wore other, less medieval, less archaic, perhaps less theological, but no less romantic colours.

What, then, was the secular background of the Crusades? I have mentioned that rural Europe, in its utter pulverization in the eighth century, possessed two social cells—if I may use that metaphor—in which its vitality could be preserved and defended. One was the monasticism of St Benedict, based originally on a simple, self-contained economy, sustained and sanctified by a religious impulse, and proof against all but total destruction. The other was the feudalism which found its distinguishing character in the time of Charles Martel: the social and military unit based on the heavily armed, well-mounted, stirruped horseman, sustained by grants of land and military tenures. Both of these units, obviously, were capable of great abuse. Monasticism, in its abusive form, would counterbalance all the temporal advantages of Christianity. It would be the means by which every corruption entered the Church. Feudalism would become a repressive, anarchical system, stifling economic growth, and leading to perpetual military faction. But these were corruptions of the original ideal. In their ideal form both monasticism and feudalism had a sense of purpose. To achieve that purpose they only needed organization. If the monastic units could be organized as a system, if the feudal units could be co-ordinated for action, and if the two systems could work together, then it was possible that the combination of ideology and military technique might, as it has done since, carry through a revolution and alter the balance of the world.

In the eighth century, when Charles Martel and his successors laid the foundations of knighthood and brought the monks of the Far West into France, Germany and Switzerland, this new organization, this new unity, already seemed at hand. In fact it was not, as yet. The Carolingian dawn was not followed by full day, and in the later ninth and tenth centuries the increasing splendour of Arabic civilization was set off by the continued darkness of Europe. Why this was so, I cannot say. Perhaps the economy of Europe could not yet sustain an effective feudalism: Charles Martel, after all, had had to confiscate land to found it: he had based it on capital, not income. Perhaps every new institution needs time to be digested; and the ninth and tenth centuries were anyway troubled times, with renewed invasions, by the Magyars on land and by the Vikings and Saracens at sea. At all events, in the tenth century neither monasticism nor feudalism showed much capacity to re-create the society of Europe. Emperors could not continue the work of Charlemagne, nor popes the work of St Gregory. Indeed the tenth-century popes have caused some embarrassment to devout historians who have to record that the papal crown was bestowed by or upon the successive lovers of one accomplished Roman courtesan and the successive descendants of another (thus justifying the medieval fable of the female Pope Joan, so dear to Protestant enthusiasts), and that the gallantries of one of them—I leave you to guess whom I am quoting—'deterred the female pilgrims from visiting the tomb of St Peter lest, in the devout act, they should be violated by his successor'.

But these times passed and in the eleventh century a great change came over Europe: a change which began north of the Alps. Exactly what that change was we can hardly say. Only one thing is certain in history, and that is that no historical process, or historical change, has a single cause: all depend not on simple mathematical logic but on a complex chemistry of causes. But one element in the chemical change of the eleventh century was undoubtedly a great, though to us unmeasurable, increase in population, and one cause, or at least

The fully developed medieval plou[g]

concomitant, of this increase of population was a series of technical improvements which increased the productivity of the land.

One such improvement, which has been a topic of vigorous historical controversy, was probably in the method of ploughing. The original plough used in the Middle East and the Mediterranean was a light 'scratch-plough', a downward-pointing spike drawn by two oxen, first in one direction, then crosswise, over a square plot of land. This was sufficient for those light, dry soils. But on the damp, heavy soil of northern Europe such a plough was inadequate except for light, well-drained uplands. Consequently agriculture was at first applied only to very limited areas. But gradually, in the Dark Ages, a new type of plough became general in northern Europe. This was a heavy plough with a coulter and ploughshare set to cut into the earth and a 'mouldboard' to turn the sod sideways and form a ridge and furrow, thereby draining as well as digging the ground. This heavy 'German' plough was often set on wheels and drawn by a team of oxen; it therefore ploughed a long strip rather than a square field. The team of oxen required communal ownership and therefore entailed, with strip-farming, a new social unit. The ultimate result of its use was greater agricultural productivity and greater

ox-team, ploughshare and mouldboard (an illumination from the Luttrell Psalter)

social cohesion. But of course it could not be adopted all at once. In fact it seems to have become general in northern Europe by the tenth century, and to have coincided with several other changes, such as the use of modern harness, the replacement of oxen by horses for traction, and the three-field system of crop rotation, all of which increased both the area and the productivity of cultivable land.

These agricultural innovations could sustain a certain increase of working population. But an increase in population is never nicely calculated, and in fact, in a generation of opportunity, the larger families which survive infant mortality will always, when they grow up, press too heavily even on expanded means of production. In the eleventh century Europe north of the Alps could not sustain the whole increase of its population, and so, on every frontier, the pressure grew. At the same time, those two preservative and aggressive institutions which Europe had found for itself discovered a new vitality, a new unity. The reforming zeal of the English and Irish monks was taken over by the monks of Cluny in France, who sought to colonize and, by colonizing, to rescue and control the Church. Where the Benedictine abbeys had been equal, independent foundations, the Cluniac houses were a disciplined, organized system, controlled from the top, from the abbey of Cluny itself, and so capable of a united policy in the Christian world. The institution of feudalism was taken over by the Norman invaders of France who used it to conquer kingdoms and fiefs for themselves and their followers in Italy and England.

It was in Italy that the two forces, always allied in society, met in politics. In 1059 the papacy, already influenced by the ideas of Cluny, allied itself with the Norman adventurers in South Italy. Seven years later it was with the blessing of a reforming pope that William of Normandy, with his small band of invincible, horsed, stirruped knights, conquered in one day the un-feudal kingdom of England. A generation later it was the same alliance of a reformed papacy and Norman feudal knights from France, England and South Italy, which sought to create new kingdoms in the East. The pressure of population forced the pace; the new institutions provided the ideology, the technique, the leadership. And in the end the ideology, as always, was adaptable: what was constant was the expansion, the conquest. The crusaders who justified their aggression against the Moslems by their virtuous detestation of the false prophet, Mahomet, did not falter when that pretext failed. The Anglo-Saxons were

76 Castle Rising, Norfolk: one of the strongholds by which the Norman conquerors perpetuated their rule in England

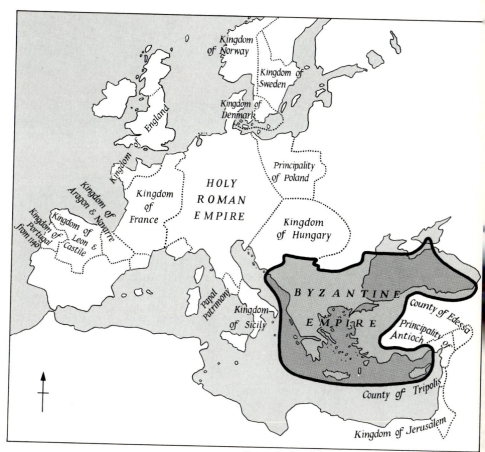

77 Europe after the First Crusade

Christian; so were the Irish; indeed Anglo-Saxons and Irish, in the past, had been among the makers of Christian Europe. That did not save the former from William the Conqueror nor the latter from Strongbow. The Greeks of Constantinople were Christians too. That did not save them from those terrible Franks, that army of land-hungry younger sons and superfluous peasants who swarmed out, to the West as well as to the East, in search of earthly as well as spiritual salvation.

Everywhere it is the same. Let us turn from the eastern to the western Mediterranean, from the north to the south Atlantic coast of Europe. In the ninth and tenth centuries, Moslem Spain, like the rest of Islam, enjoyed its golden age. While the caliph of Córdoba built the magnificent mosque there, the relics of independent Spanish Christendom cowered in northern pockets of the peninsula, worshipping in low, cavernous churches, barrel-vaulted like crypts. But in the next century, here too, we find a new Christian pressure; and once again it comes from outside, from the north. It was the monks of Cluny and the knights from France who gave form and spirit to the movement. It was the monks of Cluny who organized the pilgrimages to the great shrine of Santiago de Compostela on the remote north-west tip of Spain. They turned Santiago—the apostle St James, the brother of Jesus—into the military, crusading, patron saint of Christian Spain, and made the road to Compostela one of the great pilgrim routes of Europe; and from the beginning it was

Frenchmen who ran the hotels along the route. The petty kings of Christian Spain welcomed these enterprising immigrants, gave them lands, made them bishops in Spain. With the monks and the *hôteliers* came the feudal knights, Normans and Burgundians, to animate the 'Re-conquest'—that is, the war to recover the rest of Spain from its Moorish conquerors. Ten years before the First Crusade, it was with Burgundian soldiers that the Christians had captured Toledo; and a Frenchman was made bishop of it. It was with Norman soldiers that they twice captured the great Aragonese fortress of Barbastro. And other foreigners came too. Fifty years later a party of English and Flemish crusaders, sailing towards the Mediterranean to join the Second Crusade, arrived at the mouth of the river Douro. They were easily persuaded that there was no need to sail farther. There were infidels in Portugal, and lands as rich as any in Palestine. The crusaders agreed. They stayed. Instead of Edessa they captured Lisbon; and having massacred the Moslem

78, 79, 80 Medieval pilgrimages. (*Opposite*) The Abbey of Cluny, mother-house of the Cluniac monasteries which organized many of the expeditions. (*Below left*) The pilgrims' reward: reception into Abraham's bosom (twelfth-century tympanum detail from Autun). (*Below right*) The palace of Diego Gelmirez, first archbishop (1100–1130) and rebuilder of the cathedral of St James at Santiago de Compostela, one of the greatest pilgrim shrines

inhabitants and installed themselves on their lands, they forgot about the Christian kingdom of Jerusalem and founded—with immense, undreamed-of consequences—that of Portugal.

Italy, England, Palestine, Spain, Portugal: in all directions the frontiers of Christendom are being pushed forward. In Germany, too, we can see it. In the eighth century, the Englishman St Boniface had converted the Germans by preaching to them, and Charlemagne had converted the Saxons by knocking them on the head; but beyond the Elbe lay the world of the Prussians and the 'Slavs', those conveniently heathen sub-men who hitherto had passed through the pages of history, as they passed through the Christian kingdoms, only as long coffles of marketable eunuchs and slaves, heading for Moslem lands. In the early tenth century we find German colonists and missionaries pressing forward into the land of the Slavs and new bishoprics being founded on the Elbe; but fifty years later the Slavs have risen in revolt and all the work is undone. In the East, as in the West, the effort of Carolingian times cannot be sustained. Advance is followed, at least temporarily, by retreat.

Yet, in the next century, the advance is resumed. And, once again, it is barons and churchmen who lead the way, confident that from the pressing population behind them they will always have hands for the task. Soon they will have another instrument too. The Germans who have gone as crusaders to the Holy Land have been formed into a military order, the Order of St Mary's Hospital at Jerusalem, known as the Teutonic Knights. When opportunities in the Holy Land run short, the Teutonic Knights will be transferred to this northern theatre and will end as a rich, colonial aristocracy, a master race on the shores of the Baltic. The crusading movement is indivisible—against Moslems in the Mediterranean, pagans in eastern Europe, schismatic Christians in Byzantium, heretical Christians in the south-west of France, orthodox Christians in England and Ireland. It is indivisible because the real causes are not religion; religion only consecrated and canalized a great movement of social expansion.

But if Europe, swollen by an increased population, inspired by the Church and armed with feudal institutions, is everywhere pressing forward its frontiers, what are the means of colonization? What organization occupies and exploits the land? In part, it is the abbeys. The monastery, that cell into which the rural economy of Europe withdrew from the wrack of the Roman Empire, is now expanding again; and everywhere, under the protection of feudal institutions, it is being carried forward as an essential part of advancing Christendom. But as times have changed, the monastery too has changed, both in form and in function. In the new age of expansion the monastery is no longer a receptacle for fugitive civilization, retreating on to its narrowest base to preserve something of life, something of culture, from advancing barbarism. Far from it. It is now a pioneering, colonizing institution, the economic organism of a conquering society. And as such it has changed its form. Always, at every stage of civilization, old organs are adjusted or replaced and new movements either take over the machinery of the past or build afresh. In the darkening, defensive days of the sixth century, the Benedictine monastery had been the cell of Christendom: every cell independent, so that if one failed, another might survive. In the iron years of resistance, in the tenth century, the Cluniac monasteries had worn another form, a disciplined hierarchy. In the new, expansive era of the Crusades, yet other orders appeared: and they appeared, naturally enough, not in Italy, the Italy of St Benedict, the heart of the old Roman Empire whose extremities were failing; but in the centre and source of the new expansion, the power-house of the Crusades, the lands north of the Alps.

The greatest of these new monastic orders was the order of Cîteaux, the Cistercian order. Its effective founders were Stephen Harding, the English abbot of Cîteaux, and—appropriately enough —St Bernard, preacher of the Second Crusade. The success of the new movement was immediate. All over Europe, in the twelfth century, its abbeys sprang up. Moreover these new abbeys were not like the old abbeys. The old Benedictine abbeys, like all old foundations, had become lax and comfortable. The new Cistercian abbeys —and others, like the Premonstratensian, which followed their pattern—were stricter and more puritan. They were also up-to-date in economy and purpose. They were organized for advance, for

121

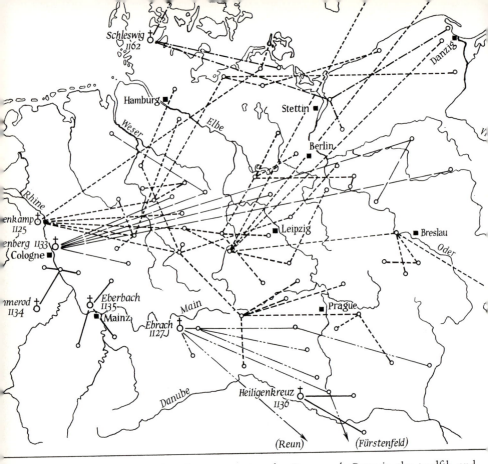

Schleswig
1162

Hamburg

Weser

Elbe

Stettin

Berlin

Rhine

enkamp
1125

enberg 1133

Cologne

merod
1134

Eberbach
1135

Mainz

Ebrach
1127

Main

Leipzig

Breslau

Oder

Prague

Danube

Heiligenkreuz
1136

(Reun)

(Fürstenfeld)

81 German Cistercian monasteries: the *Drang nach Osten* in the twelfth and thirteenth centuries. The networks of colonies sent out by the various principal houses are differentiated where necessary by the style of their connecting lines

colonization. They were centrally controlled, and yet flexible: each house sent out its own colony, and that colony would then send out another, always pushing forward in the wake of feudal power, opening up new lands. The Cistercian monks are essentially great agricultural exploiters, great cattle-raisers, and, in forward areas, colonizers of the waste. We find them in Brandenburg and Pomerania and on the Baltic coast, where the Slavs were yielding to the Germans; we find them in the wake of the German *Drang nach Osten* in Poland, Bohemia, Hungary; and we find them—at Rievaulx and Jervaulx, Fountains and Furness, Melrose and Dundrennan, Tintern and Strata Florida—in the Yorkshire valleys and on the Scottish and Welsh borders: wherever there was waste to cultivate and forest to clear.

82 Fountains Abbey, Yorkshire: one of the Cistercian houses which multiplied so rapidly during the twelfth century

But if abbeys were one organ of colonization, another, ultimately far more important, was towns. Those towns, which had almost disappeared from western Europe with the decline of the Roman Empire, began again, with the Crusades, a sudden development. They did not begin because of the Crusades. Indeed, at the beginning, the Crusades were a positive setback to the Italian towns which lived by innocent commerce with Constantinople and the Moslem cities of the Mediterranean. The Norman conquest ruined Amalfi and damaged Bari. Venice was at first a reluctant crusader. But as the Crusades went on, requiring constant sea-transport and financial refreshment, the coastal towns of Italy saw their opportunity. They provided the transport, they invested the funds, they secured payment in concessions of every kind—their own quarters in captured seaports, privileges and monopolies of trade, farms of taxes—until, in the end, they became the living, thriving link whereby Europe was once again in regular contact with the East. First on the coast

83, 84 New commercial contacts with Islam. (*Left*) Late thirteenth-century relief of the port at Pisa, whose architecture shows unmistakable signs of eastern influence. (*Right*) Text of the Treaty of Tunis (1270), an agreement for peace and mutual trade between the Moslem ruler of Tunis and the Christian kings Philip III of France, Charles of Sicily and Thibaud of Navarre

of Italy—Venice, Genoa, Pisa, Naples—then behind the coast—Florence, Milan—then along the trade-routes which ran into Central and Northern Europe—over the Alps into Switzerland and South Germany, down the Rhine to Flanders, the economic capital of the North—a vivifying impulse ran through the cities of Europe. Because the cities of Italy were enlivened by the touch of the East, they were able to stretch out their tentacles to the north also; Venice reached northwards, through the Alps into Austria, and Milan into Switzerland; Bohemia and Germany found themselves in distant touch with the Mediterranean; and Italian factors in Bruges and Ypres would buy wholesale, for Florentine manufacturers, the wool grown by the new Cistercian monasteries of England.

Moreover, thanks to the trade of the Mediterranean, and an industry financed by it, the Italian towns drew back into Europe the essential motor of such commerce: gold. Since the time of Charlemagne, as we have seen, gold had been scarce in Europe, and the western European rulers had minted no regular gold coins. The few exceptions to this rule only prove it: they were the half-arabized princes of Sicily and Spain on the borders of Islam, the Viking grand dukes of Kiev who supplied Islam with slaves, and the Anglo-Saxon King Offa who copied Arab models. But after the Crusades, all this changed. Once again the gold of Africa found its way copiously into Europe. From the Sudan it was brought by the caravans of the Sahara to the Barbary ports and thence traded to the Italian cities. Or it was sucked by trade or conquest from Constantinople, Syria, Egypt. From these new supplies the European States, after 500 years, could now mint their own gold coins. Florence led the way, minting the gold *florin* in 1252; then the other cities of Italy and France followed. In 1284 the duchy of Venice minted the *ducat*. In the next century the whole continent was once again using gold coins, the essential means of long-distance trade and high civilization.

The Italian cities profited by the Crusades; but the long-distance trade which they handled would not have reached such proportions, or had such effect, had it not been for the larger movement which lay behind the Crusades: the growth of European population and the colonization of new lands or waste lands by feudal conquest or agricultural settlement; and this larger movement also led directly to another and different form of urban development: the growth of old towns at home and the foundation of new towns beyond the old frontiers of settlement. For the European advance in the crusading period is not merely conquest and exploitation. (In some places it is. It is in the Levant. That is why the Levantine conquests were so short-lived. The crusaders were a numerically feeble ruling class, always liable to be absorbed or evicted by the more numerous natives over whom they ruled.) But elsewhere conquest is followed by settlement: the settlement not merely of new landlords imposed on a native peasantry, but of a whole society in depth; and that new society needed, for its supply and cohesion, new towns. In Spain, the advancing Christian kings everywhere set up new towns. Sometimes the kings themselves, or abbots or lay lords organize the re-population; sometimes it is left to the old towns to create new ones in their own image. In Germany, the old towns of the west,

85 'Frankish' domination in Greece: the thirteenth-century castle of Karytaina, built by Geoffrey de Brières. (A painting by Edward Lear)

which began as settlements of miscellaneous population taking advantage of the protection of a castle or a bishop's palace, acquire a new wealth, a new mercantile spirit and civic independence: the lord and the bishop shrink, the city government asserts itself. And behind the eastern advance the towns follow. The feudal lords want to set up new towns, as in Spain. The old towns send out urban colonies to supply them, just as the Cistercian monasteries also send out monastic colonies. Cologne founded Freiburg. Regensburg restored the desolate Roman city of Vienna. Lübeck planted a string of German towns on the Baltic coast and islands to open up and control the fur trade of Russia. In Brandenburg, Pomerania and Rugen alone, one hundred new towns had been founded by 1300.

My point is that the Crusades were not just a religious movement —whether we regard them as a heroic movement or an 'epidemical folly'. They were not even, by themselves, the cause of the European break-through. They were part of a much larger, much wider process: a process which can be seen all over Europe and on all the frontiers of western Christendom: beyond the Pyrenees, beyond the Elbe, on the Scottish border, in Ireland. This process is essentially a north European process. It is based on a new population-growth and new techniques, agricultural, social, military. The heavy German iron plough drives the wooden Slav plough before it beyond the Elbe, just as the heavy, stirruped, Norman knights drive the Anglo-Saxon or Celtic footmen before them in England and Ireland, and the new Cistercian monasteries press forward against the empty wastes of the Welsh and Scottish borders, the Pomeranian plain and the Baltic seashore. The towns, and the rising prices which accompany the growth of trade, do more than the Crusades to dissolve the 'feudal' power of rural knights. Perhaps, as Gibbon wrote, the Crusades were a diversion of this great expansion into the sideline of unprofitable imperialism; perhaps the imperialism was inseparable from the expansion. That is another question.

Moreover, when we look at this movement in the perspective of time, we see another thing. The Crusades were no more isolated in time than in substance. They are not a unique, unrepeatable episode. In particular combination of detail of course they are unrepeatable. No historical situation is ever exactly repeatable. But in general character they are a social phenomenon which has occurred often in history and will occur again, very shortly, even in European history. We only have to look closely to see it. The adventurers who carved out estates for themselves in the Levant, and whose grim castles still dominate the hills of Syria and scowl, impossibly alien, down the romantic valleys of Greece; the sugar plantations which the Venetians and Genoese established in the conquered islands, and the slave-labour by which they worked them; the monopolies thereby created and the spectacular fortunes of the Italian maritime cities which rested thereon—are not all these familiar at another time too?

We think of the later conquest of America. It too was a crusade. Just as the monasteries of Cluny directed the conquest of the Levant, so the great Jeronymite monasteries of Spain directed the conquest of America. For that conquest too was to be a 'spiritual conquest'. Monks and friars would accompany it and animate it, preaching down the false gods, smashing down their temples, and studding the New World with gigantic convents, granaries for the new harvest of souls. If the discovery of the Holy Lance and the True Cross inspired the crusaders in the East, Santiago on his white horse would appear to encourage the conquistadors in the West. He was '*Santiago Matamoros*'—St James the Moor-killer—but he would do to kill Red Indians too. To America also Spaniards and Portuguese would transplant all the techniques which had been developed four centuries before in the Levant. Hernán Cortés would bring to Mexico the sugar-industry which had been practised since the Crusades in the Venetian and Genoese colonies of the eastern Mediterranean. Slave-labour on the plantations and in the mills, first applied in those Levantine conquests, would become the 'peculiar institution' of the new continent. In many ways the islands of the eastern Mediterranean, now abandoned to the Turks, must have served their purpose as experimental farms for the vaster exploitations in the western hemisphere. And in the two movements, the colonization of the East in the twelfth century and the colonization of the West in the sixteenth, the spiritual and economic motives would be equally mixed. We came to America, wrote Bernal Díaz del Castillo, the companion of Cortés, as he rested on his conquered estates in Guatemala, '*para servir a Dios y hacernos ricos*'—to serve God and become rich. The inducement to the earlier crusades had been exactly the same. Come to the East, cried the Norman conqueror Bohemond, take the cross, save the tottering principality of Edessa for Christ, and get yourselves strong castles and rich cities and lands. And in Germany, at a great gathering at Merseburg in 1108, the same rewards were offered to those who would cross the Elbe and make war on the pagan Slavs: 'the country is excellent, rich in meat, honey, feathered game and flour. Therefore come hither, you Saxons and Franconians, Lorrainers and Flemings, for here two things can be won together: salvation for your souls and settlement on the best lands.'

Even the literature of the two periods is similar. The crusaders of the eleventh and twelfth centuries lived, intellectually, on the high-strung, heroic melodramas of the *Chansons de geste*—the Song of

Roland, the Song of the Albigensian crusaders: melodramas which would be brought down to earth by the pedestrian, commonsense Spanish author of the Poem of the Cid. The conquistadors of the sixteenth century lived on the equally high-strung, heroic melodramas of the 'romances of chivalry': Amadis of Gaul, Palmerín de Oliva, Sergas de Esplandián: melodramas which would be brought down to earth by the exquisite Spanish irony of Cervantes. Some of the results were the same too. If the crusaders presented Europe with leprosy, the conquistadors, not to be outdone, presented it with syphilis.

That, however, was long in the future. No one could have predicted it in the thirteenth century; less still in the fourteenth. For before the close of the thirteenth century Europe's first essay in expansion was over: over, it might seem, for ever. The wonderful generation of the Cistercians was over. The colonization of the waste had begun to slacken. Population, or at least the rate of its increase, was falling off. The world, once again, was the world of the nomads, as it had been in the seventh century; and as for the conquered empire and conquered kingdoms in the Levant, they had all gone. In Gibbon's famous phrase, 'a mournful and solitary silence prevailed along the coast which had so long resounded with the World's Debate'.

86 The seal of the Knights Templars, showing two knights riding on the same horse, symbolizes the order's original claim to poverty and humility. Its wealth and pretensions led to its suppression in 1312

V THE MEDIEVAL RENAISSANCE

Historical change is indivisible. When there is great social and political convulsion there is great intellectual convulsion too. The two centuries from 1050 to 1250 were a period of great social dynamism. We have seen the 'explosion' of population, the exploitation of new resources, and the sudden expansion of feudal, monastic Christendom over the English Channel, over the Pyrenees, over the Elbe, into the Byzantine Empire, into Palestine. They were also centuries of great intellectual excitement. The new dynamism, of which the Crusades were only one expression, had already, even before the Crusades, generated a new intellectual movement. Indeed, it may be said that in one sense the Crusades themselves were an attempt by the Church to divert and exploit that movement; but they ended by increasing its force, even against the Church. Unexpectedly, unintentionally, they brought parochial, self-centred Latin Christendom into contact with new worlds, and that contact produced a ferment in Europe. That ferment has been called 'the Renaissance of the twelfth century'.

To some people this whole concept will be strange. The nineteenth-century historians recognized only one Renaissance, the Renaissance of the fifteenth century, the Renaissance discovered and made permanent in our vocabulary by Michelet and Burckhardt. Twentieth-century historians have ended all that. The revival of ancient letters, they have pointed out, was not single or sudden: Christian Europe absorbed Antiquity not in one great bite but in several nibbles interrupted by slow periods of silent digestion. I have compared the Crusades with the conquest of America and the discovery of the East in the sixteenth century. In the same way the Renaissance of the twelfth century can be compared with the Renaissance of the fifteenth. Moreover, like the fifteenth-century Renaissance, it was accompanied by a movement of intellectual and

87 A twelfth-century schoolroom scene, apparent

religious reform which elicited, out of the old structure, a movement of reaction. There was a thirteenth-century Reformation and a thirteenth-century Counter-Reformation: a Counter-Reformation which, in its later stages, would become more complete, and therefore more blighting to progress, than that of the sixteenth century.

Renaissance, Reformation, Counter-Reformation—all these forces sprang out of the existing structure. Therefore let us glance at that structure. To have given birth to such exciting movements it cannot, clearly, have been simple. It must have been full of tensions, of complexity, of vitality.

ing lesson, illustrated in a contemporary psalter by Eadwine, a Canterbury monk

Admittedly, this is not how we see it at first glance. At first, when we look at the crusading period, we see only unanimous orthodoxy. The 'reforming' popes, with their high claims, direct the movement; the Norman and German knights, responding to the call, give it substance and force; Italian cities finance it; the Cistercian abbeys push forward at the frontiers; the towns send out their colonies. It is a movement in which all classes, it seems, are happily united in a new-found ideological harmony. The ultimate authority is never in doubt. 'By me kings reign', declares the pope—it is the theme-song of the popes at the time—as he deposes unorthodox rulers and awards their lands to hungry, predatory, orthodox adventurers; and the adventurers naturally do not question his title. Wherever they advance, feudal, monastic institutions advance with them. Gigantic new castles assert their power abroad; soaring new cathedrals—very different from the squat, cowering churches of Anglo-Saxon England or Visigothic Spain—rise out of the ground at home, from Palermo to Kirkwall; and through the *Chansons de geste* runs the arrogant, unquestioning refrain, '*Chretiens unt dreit e paiens unt tort*'— Christians are right and pagans are wrong. Schismatics and heretics, of course, are wrong, too: perhaps even wronger.

But this first glance of course gives only a superficial view. Such periods of loud unanimity, when all classes of society, suddenly reunited, outbid each other in shrill protestations of orthodoxy, seldom last long. They cannot. Society is not constructed like that. The very shrillness conceals an inner uncertainty. And in fact the Crusades were launched by a society which found harmony only in those profitable adventures. Elsewhere it was full of disharmony. The disharmony was essentially between clergy and laity, and in the course of the past century it had been sharpened into a political struggle at the summit, between popes, making new claims, and emperors, clinging to old.

The claims of the pope were double. First, he claimed that throughout society, in all matters which could be classed as spiritual, the clergy was superior to the laity, the clerical magistrate to the lay magistrate. Secondly, he claimed that the Church, in its political form, was a monarchy, and that he was the monarch. Separately these claims were, to say the least, novel; put together they meant, incidentally, that the pope was superior to the emperor. They were therefore not only novel in themselves but outrageous in their implications.

I have said that these claims were novel in themselves. Originally the Church had not been a monarchy. Originally the pope had only been one bishop out of many, with rights no greater than theirs. Even the title 'pope' did not raise him above them: other bishops also were called 'popes'. Of course the bishop of Rome was an important bishop, for Rome was a historic, populous city, visited by

St Paul and—allegedly—by St Peter. But there were other such cities, no less important: Antioch, the seat of the first Christian Church; Alexandria, the intellectual capital of the Empire; Carthage, the see of St Cyprian; Hippo, now Bône in Algeria, the see of St Augustine who had snapped his fingers at the bishop of Rome. The bishops of these sees regarded the bishop of Rome as an equal. Moreover, in Roman days, there had been no question of the clergy being superior to the lay magistrates. All the bishops had been not only equal, but equally subjects of the emperor, who confirmed, and often determined their election. Even when the Western Empire ceased, the authority of the Eastern emperor in Constantinople was still recognized by the bishops of the Church, even in the West. We have seen Pope Gregory the Great grovelling to the usurping emperor Phocas. Justinian treated the pope, as he treated the eastern bishops, very roughly: he regarded the archbishop of Ravenna, not the bishop of Rome, as the spiritual leader of Italy. Under the emperor, the supreme authority of the Church was exercised by councils in which the bishop of Rome was only one prelate among many. Such had been the system on the eve of the Moslem conquests: those conquests which, here as elsewhere, had marked a fatal term.

For when the Moslems had swept through Asia and Africa, it was not only the nutritive cities of the Empire which had been torn away from Christendom: it was also the great historic bishoprics, the rivals of Rome. Gone was the archbishopric of Antioch; gone was the partiarchate of Alexandria. Gone were Carthage, Hippo, all the 250 bishoprics of Africa, the great bishoprics of Spain. And of course, among the more modern, rural bishoprics of Europe, the bishop of Rome felt himself relatively much more important. He became, by default, the spiritual leader of Christendom; and feeling his new status, he began to pay less and less attention to the emperor in Constantinople. He also paid as little as he could to the new emperors of the West, the successors of Charlemagne. It was unfortunate for him that, theoretically, the new Western Empire was continuous with the old and retained all the old rights. It was also unfortunate that everywhere the lay princes and lay barons had established local control over the Church, and that even the pope of Rome was—and would long remain—physically at the mercy of petty nobles who could appeal to imperial authority. It was out of this situation that the tension between Church and State, clergy and laity arose.

The tension was sharpened by the difference of culture between clergy and laity. In a civilized society some lay control of the clergy is essential. It is the only thing which keeps the clergy within the bounds of sense. But in a barbarous society, where the clergy may be the only educated class, such lay control can stifle all culture. Between the end of the Roman Empire and the eighth century, western European society, from being civilized, had become barbarous. The balance of culture between laity and clergy had therefore changed. It had not changed in Byzantium. There lay culture throve, and emperors appointed cultivated laymen to high places in the Church. Such a layman was Photius, the ninth century patriarch of Constantinople—'the execrable Photius' as he was called at Rome, partly for being a layman. Photius was a distinguished scholar and patron of letters who, among other things, saved the Greek classics from extinction. Finding the Byzantine Church troubled by turbulent monks, he reduced them to order by making them copy out ancient texts. To this fortunate imposition we owe many a profane masterpiece. But in the West lay culture had collapsed, and there lay control had far less laudable results. At the summit, successive popes were made at the will of elderly courtesans and, throughout the Church, benefices were at the disposal of illiterate local magnates.

Against this lay control and lay penetration the churchmen of the West soon protested, and their protests led them to demand not only clerical freedom but, as its basis, clerical reform. In the tenth century the monks of Cluny demanded monastic reform, and to achieve it were even prepared to invoke lay power. In the eleventh century, reforming ideas penetrated to the papacy itself. In this second stage the battle was fought against the laity. The cry of these 'Hildebrandine' reformers (for their spokesman was St Hildebrand, afterwards Pope Gregory VII) was not only for reform but for

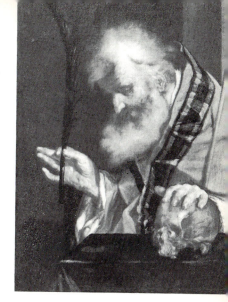

emancipation. They fought to secure ultimate control of a self-contained, independent, dominant, monarchical Church. Such a contest was a frontal challenge to the old system of the Roman Empire. It was a frontal attack on the kings who presumed that they had inherited the rights of the Roman emperors. It was an indirect attack on the emperor of Constantinople who, in the East, continued to maintain the old system and was now called schismatic for his pains.

All ecclesiastical struggles tend to be fought with doctrinal weapons and give birth to new doctrines, new forms of discipline. To detach the clergy from the laity, the popes insisted on clerical celibacy, and after a century of struggle, they succeeded in making it the rule. To raise the power of clergy over laity, they adopted new devices like auricular confession. To raise the claims of papacy to wage war in the name of a united Church, they perfected the doctrine of the Roman primacy. The Church, they declared, was ruled by a papal monarchy, not a senate of bishops. To emphasize these claims they forbade other bishops to call themselves popes. It was as absurd and impious, said one of their creatures, to suppose that there is more than one pope as to suppose that there is more than one God. To circumvent the inconvenient facts of history they

137

circulated forged documents. The most famous of these were the 'false decretals'—forged documents purporting to record decisions of the early Church—and the so-called 'Donation of Constantine', whereby the emperor Constantine, on removing his capital to the East, was alleged to have surrendered his temporal power over the western provinces of the Empire to the pope. The 'Donation of Constantine' was finally proved to be a forgery in the fifteenth century; but by that time it had done its work. The temporal power of the popes, at least in Italy, was secure and would remain secure until the nineteenth century.

So the war was fought, by fair means and foul, and in the end the popes triumphed. They triumphed because they contrived to capture the imagination and to harness the interests of men: because they persuaded men that the degradation of spiritual life was caused by lay control, and because they allied themselves with the most active elements in politics and society—with Norman feudalism, new monastic orders, new towns. The most spectacular incident in this long struggle was the humiliation of the emperor Henry IV at Canossa. At a critical moment, the emperor, the heir of Charlemagne, attempted to depose the pope. He soon found that he had over-estimated his power. Excommunicated by the pope, deserted by the German princes, he crossed the Alps in mid-winter, and after being kept waiting for three days in the outer courtyard, just to teach him his place, was admitted to the presence of the pope to do penance and receive absolution for his presumption. That was not the end of the struggle; tactically, the emperor may even have gained more than he lost by his dramatic gesture of self-abasement; but it struck the imagination of men and made the struggle itself clear and vivid. Such a struggle necessarily called forth enormous energies, and in one way the Crusades were the diversion of those energies. In the hour of apparent victory the popes saw the opportunity of using, and using up, the forces which had hitherto opposed them and which, temporarily, they seemed to have mastered. Instead of vainly and wickedly resisting the Church, they cried, let Christian princes, Christian knights accept its blessing and fight its profitable, meritorious battles abroad. The end of internal tension

89 Church and State in the eleventh century: the emperor Henry IV begs Mathilda of Tuscany and Abbot Hugo of Cluny to intercede for him with Pope Gregory VII

R ex roGat Abbatem. MaThilDiMSupplicatAtq;

often leads to external aggression. Forces and tempers, raised to a new pitch in civil strife, are united at that pitch against a foreign victim. Many foreign victims, throughout the ages, bear witness to this social truth. In the eleventh and twelfth centuries the victim was the infidel in the East; in the thirteenth it was the schismatics of Constantinople, the heretics of Albi.

But if, in this sense, the Crusades were a diversion they did not, could not, end the struggle at home; and in the new dynamism of the eleventh century that struggle took on a new form. If society was again expanding, lay culture was again in demand; and while popes were denouncing the lay control of barbarous barons, changes were occurring which made their denunciations often out of date. A new laity was being created which resented the arrogant claims of often no less barbarous priests. This new lay spirit soon found clerical leaders, and these new leaders placed themselves outside the old intellectual system. They were the professional 'masters' who, ignoring the monastic and cathedral schools—the only schools then existing—moved from place to place, like the Greek sophists of the time of Socrates, and like them, by their restlessness and emphasis on 'dialectic' or reason, excited the young and thoroughly unsettled the established teachers. These men applied their 'dialectic' to authorities already known: that is, to the Latin authors and such few Greek works as had been translated into Latin. But even that gave them enough to get themselves into trouble. For the old diehards did not like either 'reason' or profane learning. They believed that all pagan literature was by definition suspect. At least, they said, pagan literature could only be made safe by prudent excisions: was not an Israelite forbidden to marry a heathen captive, however desirable, unless she first shaved her head and pared her nails? (*Deuteronomy* XXI, 12.)

The most famous of these new 'masters' were Berengar of Tours, who in the eleventh century doubted the doctrine of transubstantiation, and Peter Abelard, the Socrates of these latter-day sophists, who dominated the first half of the twelfth century and taught his enthusiastic disciples that no book should be censured and that reason should always be heard. Berengar and Abelard were both condemned. On the other side the most famous of the diehards were St Peter Damiani, who steamed with holy rage against such idle superfluities as grammar and philosophy, and St Bernard himself, who pursued Abelard—and all other advanced thinkers—with scalding denunciations.

Thus already, before the Crusades, intellectual life was reviving in Europe, and the Crusades, which seemed at first to suspend the tensions of Christendom, to unite and exalt its rival forces, ended by bringing new material to a society which was already in a mood to grasp it. For the mere contact of societies is not enough to produce intellectual change. Societies can be receptive or unreceptive according to their social structure, social content. Some societies, like some individuals, are protected by inveterate prejudice against the possibility of learning from any contact. I do not suppose that modern Portugal, or modern Scotland, would learn much even by

90 Abelard and Héloise, master and pupil who became lovers, on a fourteenth-century carved capital in the Conciergerie, Paris

contact with the moon, though fifteenth-century Portugal and eighteenth-century Scotland were stimulated to great achievement by foreign influence. But it happened that twelfth-century Europe was receptive as well as aggressive, and the results of its contact with the East were therefore enormous. It was comparable with the equally aggressive, equally fertile contact, in the second century BC, of the unintellectual Romans with the old learning of Greece.

Indeed it was with Greece, once again—Greece, that inexhaustible reservoir of ideas through all later ages—that the contact was made. The Arabs themselves, in spite of the splendid civilization which they built up, had little of their own to offer. Even Arabic numerals, which now came to Europe, were really Indian; the Arabs were only carriers. But as carriers, their services to Europe were enormous. For when the Arabs had conquered Asia, they too had been in a receptive state, and from the Greek cities of Asia they had absorbed what 141

Arabic writer after Arabic writer would afterwards devoutly call 'the science of the Greeks'. Nor had they only absorbed it from the Greek cities. One of the great advantages of orthodoxy is the impetus which it gives to the diffusion of knowledge. Philip II of Spain by expelling the Calvinists, Louis XIV by expelling the Huguenots, Hitler by expelling the Jews, did a great deal to help the rest of the world. Similar results were achieved by two orthodox Greek emperors. First Zeno, who closed the heretical school of philosophy in Edessa, 'the Athens of Syria', then Justinian who, half a century later, closed the pagan school of philosophy at Athens itself, driving the professors of Greek philosophy to seek exile in Persia. Consequently, when the Arabs conquered Persia and ruled their huge empire—as they largely did—through a Persian bureau-cracy, they found Greek learning in fashion there too; and they hastened to acquire it. Syrian translators were employed to translate Greek science and Greek philosophy into Arabic, and all through that vast free-trade area, from Khorasan to Spain, learned men com-mented on the new Scriptures. The two Arab writers who had the greatest influence in Europe—both regarded as rather heretical at home—came from these two terminals of Islam. Avicenna (Ibn Sina) the universal genius of Islam, was a Persian from Khorasan; Averroës (Ibn Rushd), its most learned scholar, the Aristotelian who, in Dante's phrase, 'made the great commentary', came from Córdoba in Spain.

The discovery that the Arabs, as also the Byzantines, possessed the key to this new learning, soon set Europe buzzing, and to every point of contact the new 'masters' and their enthusiastic disciples set out to bring it in. One obvious point of contact was south Italy. It was now under Norman rule, but it had long been part of the Byzantine Empire, and Greek was still spoken there. There Byzantine—i.e. Roman—law had long been preserved. Thence now, it seems, came the great code of Justinian. An Italian scholar, Irnerius, lectured on it in Bologna, and another Italian, Vacarius, accompanying a Norman prelate who came to England as arch-bishop of Canterbury, taught it in Oxford. In south Italy, too, Greek medicine had survived. It had survived in Salerno, a popular

91, 92 Persian illustrations of the Greek philosophers; Aristotle, with his pupil Alexander the Great, and (*right*) a spiritual meeting of Socrates and Alexander

Roman spa south of Naples which had become famous as a medical centre in the tenth century. It was from Salerno that the work of the great Greek physicians, Hippocrates and Galen, now came to dominate medieval Europe. A second point of contact was Constantinople itself, where the merchants of Venice and Pisa set up their counters. In their wake came translators—James of Venice, Moses of Bergamo—to turn Greek philosophers and Greek Church fathers into Latin. Other translators followed the crusaders direct to Syria. But the greatest of all centres was Spain, where the archbishop of recaptured Toledo kept a school of translators at work and the Spanish Jews, who a century ago had shuttled European slaves to Islam, now went into reverse and supplied Arabic versions of Greek writers to Christendom.

143

بسم الله الرحمن الرحيم ۛ وما توفيقي الا بالله

جوامع المقالة الاولى من كتاب جالينوس في المعجونات وهي التي يذكرها هنا

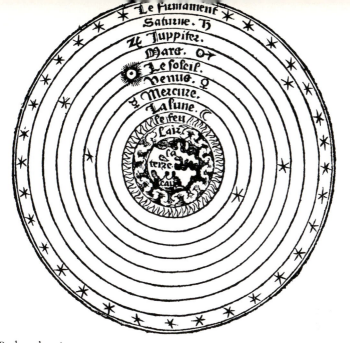

Le firmament

Saturne. ♄

Juppiter. ♃

Mars. ♂

Le soleil.

Venus. ♀

Mercure. ☿

La lune. ☽

le feu

Laer

La terre

Laū

94 Ptolemy's universe: geocentric, with the 'spheres' of earth, air, fire, the moon, the sun, five planets and the fixed stars (from a sixteenth-century diagram)

On all these points of contact scholars converged from all northern Europe. There was the Englishman, Adelard of Bath, the most widely travelled of them, who went to Spain, Sicily, Syria, Palestine; and there was the Italian Gerard of Cremona, who went to Spain to seek Ptolemy's *Almagest* and stayed to translate seventy other works. There was the Austrian, Hermann of Carinthia, who recovered Ptolemy's planisphere, and another Englishman, Robert of Chester, who translated the Arabic *Algebra*; and a host of others through whom there came to Europe—darkened indeed by successive layers of translation and opaque crusts of commentary—'the science of the Greeks': the philosophy of 'the new Aristotle'—that is, the scientific works of Aristotle not previously available in Latin—the astronomy of Ptolemy, the technology of Hero of Alexandria, the mathematics of Euclid and Archimedes, the medicine of Hippocrates and Galen. Even an abbot of Cluny entered the game, having the Koran translated—in order to refute it.

145

Galen, the medical oracle of the Middle Ages, was a Greek doctor at the court of ~~cus~~ Aurelius. His treatise on electuaries came to Europe in an Arabic translation: ~~page~~ carries his portrait (*bottom right*) with those of other notable ancient physicians

New intellectual movements tend to fashion new institutions. The Crusades had been the work of feudal and monastic institutions. But the ferment which they hastened undermined both of these. The institutions which gained from the ferment were the cities and the royal bureaucracies. The cities of Italy, even of the Rhineland and Flanders, which established colonies or counters in the eastern Mediterranean or in eastern Europe, now found themselves financial powers, and there rose to authority in them a cultivated class of patrician merchants, inspired with a new civic pride. Equally, Christian kings now discovered in eastern models new methods of government, which they could apply at home.

The greatest effects were felt, of course, where the contact was closest: by the Italian cities which financed and supplied the Crusades

95 A contemporary relief of the emperor Frederick II of Sicily with one of his sons, reflecting the arabized splendour of his court

96 One of Frederick II's architectu[ral] eccentricities is Castel del Mo[nte] Apulia: an octagonal structure w[ith] eight corner towers, also octago[nal]

and by the Norman or normanized rulers who led them. If the Norman barons who established themselves in Palestine soon changed their style, so did the Norman or normanized dynasties who profited from the Crusades at home. The Norman kings of Sicily became oriental princes, patrons, like the Arab rulers, of poets and philosophers. Their chanceries kept records in Latin, Greek and Arabic. Their German successor, the emperor Frederick II, 'the baptized sultan of Sicily', as he has been called, went further. Surrounded by an arabized court, with an extensive harem guarded by eunuchs, he patronized Italian poets and Arab or Hebrew scholars. Tempted by those delicious southern provinces, he abandoned Germany for the Mediterranean and sprinkled Sicily and Apulia with bizarre polygonal castles and machicolated hunting-lodges.

There, he hobnobbed in deplorable familiarity with equally sophisticated Moslems against whom he ought to have been launching crusades; thence he pursued his favourite sport, the Arabian sport of falconry, on which he wrote, with his own hand, the most learned and most magnificent of textbooks. For his sport he procured Arctic gerfalcons, fetched for him by German traders from the remote north-west peninsula of Iceland; he had wild hawks captured in Malta, and imported accomplished falconers from Arabia. Wherever he went, he was followed by his travelling menagerie, from which he presented his Arab friends with polar bears and albino peacocks, receiving in exchange objects of equal rarity: from the sultan of Egypt a giraffe, from the sultan of Damascus a complicated astronomical clock. Everything that Frederick did bore the mark of originality. His great achievement was to recover Jerusalem, after it had been lost to the infidel, by negotiation instead of war, and to be crowned king in it. This was regarded as especially outrageous by fire-eating popes; and indeed Frederick was under sentence of excommunication at the time and crusades were being preached

97, 98 Frederick II's favourite sport of falconry, carved on an ivory box made in 967 for Almaqueira, prince of Cordoba, and (*opposite*) in the late thirteenth-century reliefs on the Fontana Maggiore at Perugia

against him. The pope regarded him as a Moslem, or alternatively as an atheist, and his name never failed to elicit holy tantrums from successive vicars of Christ.

Frederick II was a law unto himself. His contemporaries called him *Stupor Mundi*. There is no parallel to him. But in his little way our king Henry II, half a century earlier, was almost as enjoyable. Nephew of two kings of Jerusalem, ruler of a variegated empire from the Cheviots to the Pyrenees, his estates ran into heretical Languedoc and his daughters married half-arabized princes in Sicily and Spain. In his reign England was fertilized by contact with Sicily; Englishmen held high offices in Sicily (one of them, Thomas Brown, has been described as the first Englishman whose name was written in Greek); and Arabic words, like *admiral*, reached England from Sicily. Henry himself was a sophisticated, polyglot patron of arts and sciences and his financial bureaucracy and legal system were the admiration of Europe. He also was in bad odour at Rome for standing up to the insufferable archbishop of Canterbury, Thomas Becket. The new wealth of the cities sustained, indirectly, these

princely bureaucracies: kings granted trading privileges and in return imposed taxes or raised loans. The pope himself, when he launched a crusade to wrench Naples and Sicily from 'the Viper's brood', as he always called the descendants of Frederick II, turned to city merchants: he was financed entirely by a group of *émigré* Florentine merchants, who then did very well for themselves as the capitalist financiers of Florence, Rome, and the new Angevin kingdom of Naples.

But perhaps the most significant novelty which rose out of the twelfth-century Renaissance was the universities. The 'masters', the 'sophists' of the eleventh century were already outside the old cathedral schools. The new material put at their disposal by the Arabs multiplied their influence and gradually there formed around them new institutions. The place in which these institutions settled was often accidental. They were not like the later universities, 'founded' by princes in their capitals—although Frederick II, always an exception, founded the university at Naples. They were not even, as a rule, in episcopal cities. They were communities which crystallized round some teacher interesting enough to draw students to him. The first of all, Bologna, grew up round Irnerius, the teacher of Roman law. Salerno grew out of the medical school there. The university of Paris, the model for the northern universities, owed more perhaps to the teaching of Abelard than to the cathedral school of Notre Dame which was its physical base. Oxford was not even a cathedral city (it was only raised to that status at the Reformation), but Vacarius taught there. Everywhere it was the teacher rather than the place that mattered. In education it always is.

As the universities depended so much on mobile teachers, they themselves were mobile too. Like the new towns, they were simply a body of men, under their own rules; and if necessary, they could migrate. They were like swarms of bees; and although they always buzzed and often stung, princes and cities were glad to catch them, and treated them tenderly lest they should swarm away again. Paris twice threatened to swarm, in 1229 and 1239. Orleans owed its fame as a school of canon law to a swarm from Paris. Padua—afterwards the greatest of all scientific universities—began as a swarm from

99 The new schools: a manuscript of 1256 records the donation by St Louis, king of France, of a house to accommodate four teachers of theology and their students

Bologna. In 1209 a swarm from Oxford settled at Cambridge and part of it stayed. I understand that it is still there, though, as Rashdall, the great historian of the universities says, 'what attracted them to that distant marsh town, we do not know'.

New bureaucratic governments, new urban life, new universities —such were the novel features of society in the time of the twelfth-century Renaissance. All these developments were at the expense of the feudal and monastic institutions which had formed the spearhead of the European break-through in the eleventh century. Yet, when we look at the succeeding two centuries, we have to check our enthusiasm. We see that the progress which they promised is not continued. Everywhere the new institutions, after a brilliant start, sink back. Instead of replacing the old organs of society, they succumb to them. If feudal institutions are no longer able to give effective force and unity to society—the western monarchies were anarchies held together by bureaucracy and by the military advance on all fronts—nevertheless the institutions are preserved, converted into venal patronage and glossed over by archaic chivalry. If the monasteries sink into conservative torpor, nevertheless they survive

151

as landlords, ever more parasitic on lay life. If the papacy cannot maintain its claims against kings, and its history becomes increasingly unedifying, nevertheless it contrives to crush every heresy. And meanwhile it brings the universities and the new learning both under control. Paris and Oxford become citadels of conservatism. Aristotle, after fifty years of condemnation by the University of Paris, is finally absorbed, transmogrified, and converted from the great stimulus into the great obstacle to intellectual progress. And the towns, under hereditary oligarchies tied by privileges and tax-farms to the state, gradually cease to be a radical force. The twelfth-century Renaissance seems, in retrospect, abortive: so abortive that the historians of the eighteenth and nineteenth centuries hardly saw it at all.

What caused this long, dull, successful reaction? In considering this, I think we must recognize that any reaction which is to be successful over a long period must have radical origins. There is such a thing as flat, dead, obscurantist reaction; but it seldom outlasts a generation. It dies with the generation which saw the changes and resisted them. On the other hand a reaction which is to last, which is to be accepted as an orthodoxy over several generations, must spring out of the same social circumstances as the progress which it resists. It must seem, at the time, another form of progress. I believe we can see the origins of the thirteenth-century reaction if we look at one of the concomitants of the twelfth-century Renaissance: heresy.

For the twelfth century is one of the great ages of heresy: heresy which is a sure sign of intellectual vitality just as ideological uniformity is a sure sign of intellectual stagnation. Heresy does not always spring from intellectual doubt; it often springs—as we have seen in the Roman and Persian empires—from social or political conditions, the opposition of classes to a ruling class or of nations to a ruling nation. But it is always sharpened by lay resentment of clerical privilege and abuses. As Thomas Hobbes wrote, in his somewhat summary way, all the changes in religion in the world may be attributed 'to one and the same cause; and that is unpleasing priests'. In the twelfth century, let us admit, the priests could be

100, 101 The rediscovery of Greek philosophy: German medieval stained glass windows of Plato (*left*) and Aristotle

very unpleasing. The 'Hildebrandine' reformers had fought for the independence of the Church, but they did not—could not—improve the quality of distant and lower clergy. They had merely converted the clergy into a disciplined party and given them the corrupting opportunities of power. And now a more literate laity, with new clerical leaders, was turning with excitement to the ancient, civilized past and finding—just as the sixteenth-century reformers would find—that the established church of their day was very different from the ancient models which it professed to imitate. How different, said cultivated officials of Henry II or Frederick II, was the established Church of Constantine, or even of

153

Theodosius, which had been kept firmly in place by the lay ruler! And how even more different, said simpler men who had no particular desire to see the abuse of power transferred from clergymen to lay officials, was the unestablished Church before Constantine, the Church of the Apostles, of the catacombs, of the persecutions: a Church without pope or feudal bishops or rich endowments or pagan doctrines or new articles calculated to increase its wealth and power! The economic expansion of Europe, the gathering in towns of literate merchants and poor but organized men—weavers in Flanders or Lombardy, miners in Bohemia or Saxony—provided listeners for such doctrines: listeners who felt that they were much nearer to the primitive Apostles of Christ than that blood-bolted bishop whose coat of chain-mail was sent by his captor to the pope with the ironical question, the question of Joseph's brethren to Jacob, 'know whether this be thy son's coat?'; or that luckless archdeacon who, having reached the Holy Land, was surprised and transfixed by the infidel while dallying in a fragrant orchard.

Such opinions are not, of course, exclusively twelfth-century opinions. They are a staple form of heresy. But in the twelfth century they were uttered more loudly, and heard more eagerly, than ever before. It was a general outburst. The particular forms which it took were various. There were men like Pierre de Bruys, who rejected infant baptism and would have turned the Church of conformists into a sect of believers, and Arnold of Brescia, a pupil of Abelard, who denounced the temporal power of the pope and found enough followers to set up a brief Roman republic. These opinions, as Hume wrote of a later thinker, 'it would seem are not orthodox, and there was a necessity of delivering the holders to the flames'. There were also men—one was burnt in Paris in 1209—who found evidence that the pope was Antichrist, and numerous sects who pursued the evangelical virtues and apostolic poverty, like the Umiliati of Lombardy and the Waldenses or Poor Men of Lyons. There were also messianic prophets who announced the imminent end of the world in remarkable detail; and ascetics who flogged themselves through populous cities, calling for repentance before that great day should come. All these sects, like the Church, were international; they were bred, as popes and bishops reluctantly confessed, by the rottenness of the international Church. To cope with the problem the Church stamped out the boldest of their leaders and sought to tame the less outrageous. Its two most signal triumphs were the stamping out of the Albigensians and the taming of the preachers of Holy Poverty, the friars.

The Albigensians were the most radical, the most ascetic, and the most universal of all the heretics. Like so many of the ideas of medieval Europe, their doctrine came from Persia: it was the old Manichaean dualism which had contended with Christianity in the fourth century and which had now returned, as a fanciful Christian heresy, after a circuitous journey through Byzantium, Armenia and Bulgaria. Thanks to devoted missionaries and a marvellous organization this heresy was suddenly found, in the twelfth century, to have honeycombed all Europe: a sure sign of a general spirit of revolt. With its own laity, its own clergy, its own bishops, its own international councils, it challenged Rome on her own ground, without the possibility of compromise. Certainly it never compromised. Its adepts always resisted to the last. 'If the blood of martyrs were really the seed of the Church', wrote the great historian of the Inquisition, H. C. Lea, 'Manichaeism would now be the dominant religion of Europe.' But as long as these Manichaean heretics were scattered over Europe, the Church felt that it could deal with them. It might not be able to crush them out, but at least they could never make frontal war on it. The really dangerous moment for the Church came when this international subversive movement found a local base and a princely protector. The local base was the area known as Languedoc, in the south-west of France. This was a peripheral area, racially distinct from northern France, and therefore a typical seat of heresy. It also happened at that time to enjoy particularly unpleasing priests. The princely protector was the count of Toulouse, 'the greatest count on earth', the equal—it was said by the troubadour poets of his gay, sophisticated court—of emperors and kings. For the established Church this was a moment as dangerous as when the duke of Saxony became the patron of Luther.

The established Church took no risks, Crusades were declared. The lands of the count were declared forfeit and were granted to the orthodox prince who would conquer them. An army of predatory Norman warriors duly descended. The heresy was smothered, and smothered finally, in torrents of blood; and by the end of the century the great new fortified cathedral of Albi and the new university of Toulouse, specially founded as citadels of the correct faith, looked out over a desolate but orthodox land.

Meanwhile another great institution was being forged: an institution which bridged the gap between heresy and orthodoxy. For that gap is not necessarily wide or deep. Most heretical movements begin within the bosom of orthodoxy, and a politically skilful Church will contrive to keep some at least of them from jumping finally out. The Church of Rome, at least in the thirteenth century, showed that political skill. The Church of Rome, as Macaulay wrote, 'thoroughly understands what no other Church has ever understood'—Macaulay never said anything less than emphatically—'how to deal with enthusiasts':

'In some sects, particularly in infant sects, enthusiasm is suffered to be rampant. In other sects, particularly in sects long established and richly endowed, it is regarded with aversion. The Catholic Church neither submits to enthusiasm nor proscribes it, but uses it. . . . Place Ignatius Loyola at Oxford. He is certain to become the head of a formidable secession. Place John Wesley at Rome. He is certain to become first General of a new society devoted to the interests and honour of the Church. Place St Teresa in London. Her restless enthusiasm ferments into madness not untinctured with craft. She becomes the prophetess, the mother of the faithful, holds disputations with the devil, issues sealed pardons to her adorers, and lies in of the Shiloh. Place Joanna Southcott at Rome. She founds an order of barefooted Carmelites, every one of whom is ready to suffer martyrdom for the Church; a solemn service is consecrated to her memory; and her statue, placed over the holy water, strikes the eye of every stranger who enters St Peter's.'

102   After the 'crusade' to exterminate the Albigensian heresy the fortified cathedr.
Albi was founded in 1277 as a citadel of triumphant orthod

103 St Dominic and St Francis, the founders of the new orders of friars, which enabled the papacy to triumph over heresy in the thirteenth century: the imaginary meeting at Incontro portrayed by Andrea della Robbia. (Fifteenth-century terracotta from the Loggia di San Paolo, Florence)

Macaulay was writing of the Counter-Reformation of the sixteenth century. He might have been writing of that of the thirteenth. Faced with the universal outbreak of heresy, the Church of Rome might use all methods to stamp out the revolt, but it also won over some of the radicals to its side. And out of their enthusiasm it obtained allies and forged institutions which would oppose heresy on its own level. Its aim was to divert the dangerous flood of 'enthusiasm', to tame and canalize its turbid waters, and in the end to refloat on those waters the creaking hulk of orthodoxy which they had threatened to break up. The secular clergy lacked time and enthusiasm for such a task. The old institutions of monasticism could not be adapted to the new purpose. The new institutions in which the papacy invested, in order to realize it, were the new orders of the friars, and the organ which, increasingly, they operated, was the Inquisition.

The two first orders of friars, the Dominicans and the Franciscans, both rose directly out of the heretical crisis of the twelfth and

thirteenth centuries. St Dominic began as a preacher among the Albigensians of Languedoc. St Francis, with his cult of Holy Poverty, recalls the Poor Men of Lyons, the Poor of Christ, and other ascetic sects. But whereas these other sects were driven or led into heresy, and even the original doctrines of St Francis were, after victory, to be declared heretical, the Church decided, in the crisis of the thirteenth century, to use these new allies who could speak to heretics in the language they understood. Moreover, thanks to these new armies, directly at its disposal and free from local administrative duties, the Church could man a new central organization for the repression of heresy: an organization which the canon lawyers hastened to supply with a formidable procedure and—a novelty in Europe—the judicial use of torture. The support which the papacy, after much hesitation, gave to the projects of St Dominic and St Francis marked the beginning of the continuous medieval Counter-Reformation, and the imaginary meeting of the two saints, one heading for Rome, the other from it, at Incontro, 'The Meeting

Place' in the Tuscan Hills, became a theme of Catholic art. Thanks to them Gibbon could write that the early thirteenth-century popes 'may boast of the two most signal triumphs over sense and humanity, the establishment of trans-substantiation and the origin of the Inquisition'.

The effects of the medieval Counter-Reformation were not felt at once. In their first century the friars were still a radical force, an intellectual *élite*. Nor must we ascribe too much to single decisions or institutions. All historical developments, including religious developments, are meaningless except in their social framework. If other forces had not conspired with them, the friars and the Inquisition could not have succeeded, as they afterwards did, in crushing and sucking the life out of medieval Christendom. Like the Crusades, the medieval Counter-Reformation must be seen as part of a process. The process which lay behind the Crusades was a general expansion. The process which lay behind the medieval Counter-Reformation was an equally general stagnation. We can see it in many fields. There is the falling-off of population-increase after 1300—it has been argued that periods of clerical domination generally coincide with falling population. There is the cessation of colonization, whether in the Levant or beyond the Elbe. There is the weakening of economic life, illustrated by the collapse of the Italian financiers which began in 1298. There is the failure of religious radicalism— after the friars, the popes saw to it that no new orders were founded till the Reformation. All these things illustrate general stagnation and it was no doubt because of that stagnation that the new institutions were able, so easily, to stifle the radical forces and the intellectual vitality out of which they too had been born. Nevertheless, within this social framework, I believe that the Counter-Reformation of the thirteenth century had as much influence in retarding the development of Europe in the two centuries after 1300 as the Counter-Reformation of the sixteenth century was to have in the two centuries after 1600. The difference was that the medieval Counter-Reformation was far more complete. There was no Protestant England or Holland. After it Christendom, checked, had to start again.

If we were to take a date to represent the highest point of the European Middle Ages, I suppose that date would be about 1250. Up to that date we see—from about 1050 onwards—only advance. There is growth of population, agricultural revolution, technological advance. The frontiers of Christendom are pushed forward in all directions; new worlds are discovered, and also old; there is a sophistication of manners, a revival of letters. New institutions are founded, both lay and spiritual: on the one hand towns and universities, on the other new orders of improving monks and missionary friars. And meanwhile, within Europe, art and literature are reviving: barbarian Europe has been captured by its more cultivated victims, just as barbarian Rome had been fourteen centuries ago.

However, as history constantly reminds us,

'everything that grows
holds in perfection but a little moment',

and from about 1300 the decline is obvious. Already in the middle of the thirteenth century the territorial expansion had been halted. In 1242 the eastward advance of the Teutonic Knights had been held up by the ruler of the Russian Slavs, Alexander Nevsky. Two years later Jerusalem, recently recovered, had been finally lost. Thereafter the pace quickened. In 1261 the Greeks returned to Constantinople. In 1263 the conquered Moors in Spain rose in a great revolt which halted the 'Re-conquest' for two centuries. In 1268 the Latin principality of Antioch was lost, in 1289 the county of Tripolis. In 1291 Acre, the last remnant of Christian rule in the Holy Land, was overpowered. By 1300 all that remained of the Eastern Empire of Christendom was a few shrinking relics of Greece: and even those were seldom held by the now bankrupt families which had conquered them. The Frankish 'families of Outremer' were being replaced by the Italian capitalists, their creditors. Venice and Genoa ruled in the Peloponnese, in Crete, in the Greek islands. Directly or indirectly, feudalism was yielding to finance. In 1311, nine years after the feudal knights of France had gone down before the Flemish townsmen at Courtrai, a generation before they would go down before the English bowmen at Crécy, the Frankish chivalry of Greece was mown down on the banks of the river Cephisus by the plebeian foot-soldiers of the Catalan company. By the end of the century the Catalans in their turn would have gone and the new Duke of Athens would be Nerio Acciaiuoli, a member of a famous family of Florentine bankers.

But if the fourteenth century saw the downfall of European chivalry, it was not easy going for the bankers either. Indeed, in the years from 1300 to 1350 the heavyweight horsemen of the financial world suffered their Courtrai, their Cephisus, their Crécy too. It was half a century of successive bankruptcies. The great Sienese banking house of the Buonsignori, 'the Rothschilds of the Middle Ages', went first in 1298. The Ricciardi of Lucca followed in 1300. The Ammanati and Chiarenti of Pistoia came next. Meanwhile economic recession had hit Florence. Dante's life was spent against a background of fierce faction in his own city, faction which would drive him into embittered exile. The next generation was punctuated by the failure of Florentine banking houses, culminating, in 1326, with the spectacular crash of the oldest and greatest of them all, the Scali. After that, only three great banking houses stood firm: they were the three newer houses of the Bardi, the Peruzzi and the Acciaiuoli, known as 'the columns of Christendom'. But they did not last long. In 1343 the tide of bankruptcies reached them. By 1346, the year of Crécy, all three were down. And, indeed, those two dramatic episodes were not unconnected. Our King Edward III stood behind them both. From behind his windmill on the field of Crécy, he watched the slaughter of the French knights, and by his default he precipitated the ruin of the Italian financiers. He was the biggest client of the Bardi and the Peruzzi, and it was his failure to pay the huge interest on his loans which caused the fatal 'run on the bank'.

The financial crisis of the fourteenth century, like that of the early

104 Unmounted bowmen
and feudal knights at the
battle of Crécy, 1346

seventeenth century, or that of the nineteen-twenties, was not self-
contained. It was part of a general crisis, a crisis of society, and—like
those later crises—it marked the end of an age: the great divide
between the age of expansion and the age of contraction, the earlier
and the later Middle Ages. Moreover, it was accompanied by
another, even greater disaster. The year after the collapse of its feudal
and financial pillars, Europe, already weakened by a series of famines,
was visited by a more general calamity: the Black Death.

The Black Death was bubonic plague, carried by black rats—
or rather, by a flea parasitic on black rats—and spread, in favourable
circumstances, in crowded, dirty, medieval towns. Once before it
had come to Europe. In the sixth century, in the reign of Justinian,
corn-ships had brought it to Constantinople, causing, in Gibbon's

163

words, 'a visible decrease of the human species, which has never been repaired in some of the fairest countries of the globe'. In the words of one great authority on the subject, this terrible plague of Justinian's time and the Black Death of the fourteenth century 'are the two greatest pestilences in recorded history; each has no parallel except in the other'. At least they had no parallel when those words were written, in 1890. The earlier plague had come from Egypt, from Pelusium, the great port of entry for the goods of Asia. Perhaps the plague had been brought from Asia too. The Black Death came from Crimean Tartary, and it was from the Genoese station of Caffa in the Crimea, which had suffered a three years' siege by the Tartars, that Genoese ships brought it to Genoa in the spring of 1347. It also came indirectly through Constantinople, which was similarly infected from the Crimea. The Crimea was the terminus of the greatest of the caravan routes from Europe to China —that is why the Genoese had built their factory there—and it is most probable that the seeds of the plague were brought thither, in the caravans, from China. China was to be the source of the third great epidemic too. This was the plague which reached Canton and Hong Kong, from the inland provinces of China, in 1894, and quickly spread to India, America and Australia. But at present we are concerned with the Black Death and its impact on Europe.

105   The Black Death: burning of infected clothes

That impact, we all know, was devastating. It was also universal. The plague struck the Mediterranean countries first. Soon after its arrival in Genoa it reached the Sicilian port of Messina. About the same time—the end of 1347—ships from Constantinople brought it to Marseilles. Thence it spread through France. In Italy *la mortifera pestilenza* of 1348, which had emptied the city of Florence and over-turned the authority of all law, human and divine, provided the setting for Boccaccio's *Decameron*. In Parma, Petrarch lamented the loss of his Laura and of many other friends. 'When will posterity believe', he asked, 'that there was a time when, without combustion of heaven or earth, without war or other visible calamity, not just this or that country but almost the whole earth was left uninhabited . . . empty houses, deserted cities, unkempt fields, ground crowded with corpses, everywhere a vast and dreadful silence?'

From Italy the plague was soon carried all over Europe. Travelling quickly by sea, it reached England in 1348, and raged there for three years. The ingenious Scots, seeing their neighbours thus prostrate, gathered gleefully in the forest of Selkirk to invade and despoil them. Their chief spoil consisted of the plague, which spread over their whole country in 1350. In Ireland, a friar of Kilkenny, having recorded the desolation around him, foresaw—correctly—that his chronicling days would soon end, and considerately left a supply of

106 Burial scene at Tournai in 1349, at the height of the Black Death

parchment for his successor, 'if haply any man survive, and any of the race of Adam escape this pestilence and continue the work which I have begun'. From Italy the plague also passed by sea to the east coast of Spain and gradually moved westwards into Portugal. From Venice it was carried through the Alps to Austria. It also went by sea to the Baltic and penetrated into Russia. From Austria, from the Baltic and from France it converged on Germany, where zealous agitators were quick to explain that it was caused by Jewish poisoning of good German wells.

The Black Death raged at its worst for three years; but even when the worst was over it still lingered in the soil of Europe. There were five severe secondary outbreaks before 1400. Nor did they end with the century. Though it gradually contracted into the great cities, the plague was domesticated in Europe till the mid-seventeenth century. The Great Plague of London in 1665 was its last English, the plague of Marseilles in 1720 its last European, eruption. After that, conditions changed. In 1727 came a new invasion from the Russian steppes. Brown rats swarmed over the Volga, displacing the black rat, with its parasites and its plague.

The immediate consequences of this terrible mortality, which carried off in some places half, in general perhaps a third, of the population, were enormous. Everywhere there was a shortage of labour. Everywhere the established classes, the beneficiaries of past expansion, sought to conserve their now threatened gains by a policy of artificial reaction. To do so they devised new legislation, new machinery, even new myths. And everywhere, equally, there was resistance. In the expanding world of the twelfth and thirteenth centuries there had been room for all and a certain unity of social classes could be preserved. Landlords had granted freedom to their serfs because the serfs had acquired money from agriculture and could buy it, or because, if it were not granted, they might run away to the freedom of the new cities. In the cities, society had been fluid: apprentices had risen to be masters and the city offices had passed from old families to new. But in the contracting world of the fourteenth and fifteenth centuries there was less room; and the lord and peasant in the country, great merchant and small—or merchant

107 A German 'plague cross', used in prayer for delive

and craftsman—in the town fought, the one to retain, the other to acquire his share of the dwindling stock of wealth or power.

The struggles did not all go the same way. In England, immediately after the Black Death, the landlords passed the Statute of Labourers, designed to peg agricultural wages at or near the rates obtaining before the plague. In France, a royal ordinance did the same. In Spain, similar regulations were issued by the *cortes* or Estates for the various regions. But ultimately, in most of these western countries, the shortage of labour gave advantages to labour, and peasants were able to buy their freedom. In eastern Europe, on the other hand, the landlords enforced their will. In the face of Slav pressure, they found means, little by little, to reimpose serfdom, so that by the sixteenth century, when the free peasantry of England boasted of their superiority to the wooden shoes and canvas breeches of the less free peasants of France, the French peasants could look with equal disdain at the serfs of Germany, sent out to gather snails and strawberries for their despotic masters. In each country the same causes led to the same 'landlord reaction'; but the outcome was different. Even in Spain there were differences between Catalonia, where the new legislation was afterwards revoked, and Castile where it was not. The same causes do not necessarily produce the same results in history; or at least, to do so, they require the same social context. Failing that context, the results may even be opposite.

Meanwhile, the towns too were in crisis. In the late fourteenth and the fifteenth centuries nearly all the established towns of Europe suffered eclipse. With the decline of population and of trade, their wealth and confidence sagged, and within them there were new struggles for privilege and power. To resolve these struggles, different factions sometimes appealed to neighbouring princes, and so the civil struggles of the towns became involved—often disastrously involved—in the foreign wars of kings. Sometimes, in their despair, the towns cannibalized their neighbours, as Florence strengthened itself by swallowing up Arezzo and Pisa, and Augsburg by squeezing out Memmingen and Ulm. And many towns, in the precariousness of trade, turned themselves into landlords. Land might bring its troubles but they were often less than the troubles of foreign trade. So the towns too became investors in the 'landlord reaction'. We see it happening in Barcelona where the city merchants switch their capital from overseas commerce to agricultural improvement at home. We see it most clearly in Venice. While the great Venetian merchants clung to their dwindling commercial empire in the Aegean sea, the lesser, weaker merchants supported a policy of conquering a *terra ferma* on the mainland. In 1381 there was a general economic collapse of the merchant houses in Barcelona, followed, in the fifteenth century, by civil war. In the same fifteenth century Venice, which had hitherto looked seawards, to the gorgeous East, turned round and fought war after war to secure territory in Italy: territory in which, in the next century, Palladio would build and Veronese decorate the majestic villas of a once mercantile aristocracy which had gradually turned from commerce to office and from office to land.

Finally, what of the Church? In these years of depression it too turned in on itself. I have already remarked that any genuine, living counter-reformation, as distinct from mere reaction, must spring out of the same forces which have produced the original reformation. The friars had begun as revolutionary, not reactionary forces: they had canalized, in defence of the Church, some of the new radicalism of the twelfth-century heretics—the ideas of apostolic poverty and missionary evangelism. But in the fourteenth century this radicalism was effectively crushed out of the Church. The friars became an extra buttress of a bureaucratic property-owning Church deprived of spiritual authority first by the 'Babylonish captivity'— the migration of the papacy from Rome to Avignon—then by the 'Great Schism', when pope and antipope, from Rome and Avignon, hurled at each other their sizzling but ineffectual spiritual thunderbolts. In 1322 Pope John XXII, the risen cobbler's son who savoured the pleasures of wealth among the delicious, specially planted papal vineyards of Avignon, condemned as heretical the doctrine of the poverty of Christ and thereafter the early lives of St Francis were re-written to tone down the unfortunate views of the founder on that subject. The popular fame of the friars of the fourteenth and fifteenth centuries was less for their poverty and their preaching than

169

To the left of and below the image, fragments of Middle English text in blackletter script are visible:

igedie
heigh degree
yaucdie
in sitee
Jft to flee
his oße

9 oße

seie
iernne

108 Chaucer's Monk waxed prosperous on the revenues of starving parish priests:
'Of priking and of hunting for the hare
Was al his lust, for no cost wolde he spare.'

for their wealth and the interesting new ways in which they built it up. The Franciscans were famous as the inventors or improvers of those 'mechanical' aids to religion which would provoke the Reformation: indulgences, fancy new devotions, new dogmas like the Immaculate Conception. The Dominicans built up their power as the formulators of orthodoxy, and as the manipulators of the Inquisition which would defend orthodoxy by crushing out every new idea.

As for the monks, if the new mendicant orders, which professed poverty, could boast so openly of their wealth, why should the old monasteries hold back? Everywhere the monasteries had extended their landed property. They too had invested in the 'landlord reaction'. The Black Death, in this respect, had been a positive benefit to them. In the years of desolation men had turned to religion and left their lands to the Church. And with land the monks also swallowed up the tithes of the parish churches. This was perhaps the greatest of all the charges levelled against them. Everywhere we read of parish churches falling into ruin and parish priests starved while monasteries enjoyed nine-tenths of their revenue. In *Piers Plowman*, that document of English discontent in the fourteenth century, we read of 'religious, that have no ruth though it rained on their altars'—for the churches which those religious should maintain are roofless with neglect. Nor was this merely an English complaint. 'There is overwhelming evidence for this kind of thing', says one of the greatest authorities on the medieval Church, 'in every European country.' The monasteries did well on the surplus of such endowments. We see the result in Boccaccio and Chaucer. Chaucer's monks and nuns are all jolly, sleek, property-loving animals: it is the starved parish priest, their victim, of whom he writes:

> But Cristes lore and his apostles twelve
> He taughte, and first he folwed it himselve.

Because of these unfashionable evangelical virtues, Chaucer's poor priest was denounced by the more worldly Canterbury pilgrims as a 'loller', a Wycliffite, a heretic.

109 The 'Wyclif Bible': opening of the *Acts of the Apostles*

For of course this 'landlord reaction', this dull, reinforced, conservatism of the established classes, did not go unchallenged. It was challenged in the country: the fourteenth century was punctuated by desperate, sometimes terrible, peasant revolts. The peasants revolted in western Flanders from 1323 to 1328. In 1357 they revolted in France: it was the famous Jacquerie, which gave its name to all other purely peasant risings. In 1381 they revolted in England: it was the great Peasants' Revolt of Wat Tyler and Jack Straw whose names remained bogeys to alarm the gentry in the seventeenth century. In the towns, too, there were risings against the closed merchant oligarchies which controlled all economic life. Between 1348 and 1400 there were numerous 'strikes'—in Paris, in Speyer, in Siena, in Strasbourg, in Constance. There were also some full-scale revolts. The two most highly developed industrial areas in Europe were Flanders and Italy. In Flanders the pace was set by the principal industrial city, Ghent. There, since the city merchants had sought the alliance of the King of France, the craftsmen sought that of the King of England, and Edward III found himself the patron of social revolution led by the tribune of the weavers, Jan van Artevelde. A generation later, Philip van Artevelde would inherit his father's mantle and lead 'the odious weavers' once more in revolt against their masters. At the same time—in 1379–82—the clothworkers of Florence led a similar revolt against the merchant oligarchy of their city. It was called the rebellion of the Ciompi. 'It would be no exaggeration to say', wrote Henri Pirenne that in those years 'on the banks of the Scheldt, as on those of the Arno, the revolutionaries sought to impose upon their adversaries the dictatorship of the proletariat.' And to sanction their revolt, peasants and craftsmen alike armed themselves against the Church of the rich with radical, heretical doctrines. In France and England the peasants attacked the great landowning abbeys and burnt their archives, the record of their own subjection; they listened to anarchical preachers of human equality like John Ball; and even unrevolutionary enemies of the Church, like Wyclif, found their doctrines turned into revolutionary slogans. Wyclif's heresies were preserved in England, especially by

communities of weavers, and would survive to give substance to the

110 Wat Tyler (*left*), at the head of the Kentish rebels, threatens Richard II with his sword but the Mayor of London intervenes: a scene from the Peasants' Revolt of 1381

Protestant Reformation of the sixteenth century. They also travelled, very quickly, to Bohemia. There they were adopted first by the Czech Hussites, who fought, under the sign of the chalice, against both clerical and German oppression; then by their extremists, the Taborites, social revolutionaries who fought to death and martyrdom and whose strength came—as in Flanders, Liège, France and Italy—from weavers and miners.

Finally, the fourteenth century saw another form of popular revolt: anti-semitism. Indebted peasants in the country, starving craftsmen in the towns, looked for scapegoats in their midst and found the Jews. The Jews were expelled from England in 1292. At the same time there were pogroms in the kingdom of Naples. In 1348–9, on the approach of the Black Death, the Jews were massacred throughout Switzerland and Germany. Popes, princes, bishops, great landlords, sought to protect them, for they found them useful;

111 Jews were the scapegoats of the late thirteenth and fourteenth centuries. Here the Jews of Cologne are burned alive during the massacre prompted by the approach of the Black Death

112 St Bernardino of Siena, friar and Jew-baiter, preaching to an Italian confraternity (fifteenth-century painting by Vecchietta)

but in vain: in city after city the Jews were rounded up and burnt alive, until, as a German chronicler wrote, 'I would have believed that the last end of Jewry had come if the time prophesied by Elijah and Enoch had been completed; but since that is not so, some must survive, that the Scriptures may be fulfilled.' In 1391, ten years after the revolutionary movement in England, Flanders and Italy, and the economic crisis in Catalonia, an equally wholesale massacre of the Jews took place in Spain. The pogroms were generally animated by the friars. The Dominican St Vincent Ferrer, the most famous of Spanish preachers, the miracle-working friar of Catalan art, inspired the massacre in Spain; the Franciscan St Bernardino of Siena, the great Observantine, whose sour puritan face stares at us from so many Umbrian churches, whipped up the faithful in Italy. Both St Vincent and St Bernardino represent the radical puritan wing of their orders. They are the second St.Dominic and the second St Francis, similar apostles of a later, but disillusioned generation.

What was the cause of this general decline of the fourteenth century, this collapse of the vitality which had sustained Christendom in the two centuries of expansion? It was not only the Black Death. Population had already begun to fall before the plague had come, and it did not recover momentum until well after it was over. The abandonment of villages beyond the Elbe had also begun well before the Black Death; so had the agrarian and urban discontent in the West. In general a healthy society soon recovers from decimation by an epidemic. London would shrug off the terrible plagues of 1625 and 1665. It is feeble societies which are fatally damaged—and which then ascribe their weakness to that cause. We cannot therefore put all the blame on the Black Death. We have to ask why European society was already so enfeebled in the fourteenth century that the impact of the Black Death was so formidable. For one reason we must look once again outside Europe, to the source whence the Black Death and so much else had come: the East.

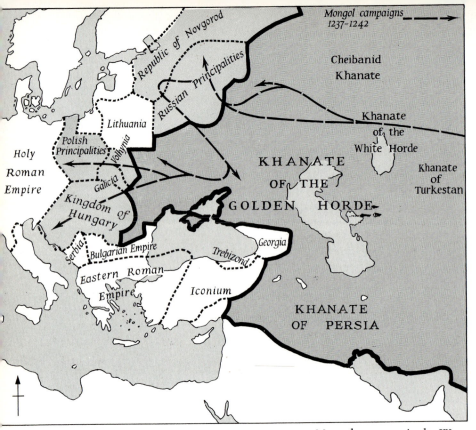

113 Mongol conquests in the West:
Europe's eastern boundary in the late thirteenth century

For these years of European reaction were years of spectacular change outside Europe; and once again, as in the days of the Huns and the Avars, the immediate cause of the change was one of those sudden, great confederations of the nomads of the steppe. This time it was the greatest of all such confederations: the Mongol confederation of Genghis Khan who, in the early thirteenth century, from his capital of Karakorum in Outer Mongolia, had created an empire of heathen conquest from the Pacific to the Volga. Under his sons and grandsons this empire was extended still farther. In the West the Mongols overthrew the principality of Kiev, sacked its capital, the cradle of Russian civilization, and subjected Russia for two centuries. Alexander Nevsky, victorious over the Teutonic Knights, bowed to these less repulsive conquerors. The Mongols invaded Poland and Hungary, burnt Cracow and Budapest. In the Middle East they captured Baghdad, abolished the caliphate which had been continuous since the Prophet, and set up a Mongol dynasty in Persia. In the East, Kublai Khan, Genghis's grandson, conquered the whole Chinese Empire, transferred his capital to Peking, and sent his armies and fleets into Burma and Java. Only distance defeated the Mongols in the West. Only the two new Turkish slave-empires— the slave oligarchy of the Mamelukes in Egypt and the slave-kings of Delhi in India—were able to resist their onslaught on Islam. Only Japan, thanks to a timely storm, escaped the eastern conquests of Kublai Khan.

To the rulers of western Europe these convulsions of Islam were not unwelcome. Here was a powerful second front against Mamelukes and Turks; here also was a huge free-trade area from Budapest to Canton; and both could be exploited. Franciscan missionaries were sent to convert the heathen khans to Christianity and Italian merchants found their way, through Central Asia, into China, 'the head of the world and the beginning of the earth'. Of the former, the most famous were Giovanni da Piano Carpini who was sent by Pope Innocent IV and arrived at Karakorum in 1245, and Guillaume de Rubrouck, sent by St Louis, King of France, who turned up in Karakorum in 1254. These missionary efforts were a failure. As Robertson says, 'the haughty descendant of the greatest conqueror Asia had ever beheld' was astonished at the 'strange mandate from the Italian priest whose name and jurisdiction were alike unknown to him'. But the mercantile expeditions were more successful. The heathen khans needed foreign experts and preferred, in their immediate entourage, not to use either Moslems or Chinese. Genghis Khan liked Uighurs, those fascinating Turks of Sinkiang, who had once been Manichaeans and who now served their conquerors by reducing the Mongol language to writing. Under him the Uighurs became the court aristocracy of Karakorum, and he appointed an Uighur as tutor to his sons. But there were also Christians. Guillaume de Rubrouck found numbers of them in

Karakorum in 1254; and when Kublai Khan established his power they began to flow to his courts at Cambalu and Peking. The first to come from Europe were two Venetian merchants, Niccòlo and Maffeo Polo, who set out from the Crimea via Bokhara to Peking. Ten years later Marco Polo, the son of Niccòlo, would begin his fifteen years as a favoured officer of Kublai Khan, and by his famous book would inspire numerous other Italian merchants to find their way to China in the years 1300–50.

Thus, when the crusaders' way of imperialist colonization had failed, the alternative way of 'pure and friendly correspondence' succeeded, and in the century after the failure of the Crusades, Europe was still living, successfully, on the East. Indeed, it was living more successfully than ever. The great, orderly, tolerant Mongol Empire, crossed and re-crossed by continual caravans, provided one of the

114   Niccòlo and Maffeo Polo, the Venetian merchants, in the presence of Kublai Khan at his court in Peking

كواب اداع كارليرى رمر

حاجم

امير من مكن بابا مسم
حاشرلى مكسر كلمر
ماطا اذا كك كثر فرمه
وكى الى الام سم معم
واكنا مس نتبرايا ماجلا ى الا لمام مسم
وبال باص ابرى لاباى اى بدلا نوم
وماط دامر ايرا لباى مدا كانه واشرله مكسم
واكرعى نوسر ما لمالك ما ما بلكرى دلا مذرده م
ك بمرم بركرى ماه ماطرى مى م لكر برده مم
بعثر واوانمام مم لكر بده م
مانرا ابرى ام ماكرى ى كى لكبر الكسم
حدوكا اعاا لى لمادهمير هر ماصر صوده م
سدكلاكرا مى كلسلمار ما ما لانهوا لصالم
الهمان ابر كا كسمار الى كمر بلانها لمرحم
ماحا سان نرم ككرا ا سه مار و رامرم كنر
وتحرجى رهكول ى رمه الرى دمسر
كى كو جرى لكم جرالى مار اى كى ماردم مم
حبام ارم رادى لى ماحر كى اى اهلم م
حكى كى لماردى ا اى ماى وادم كى ماكر برا
كى ابمرابدى ى لما كى الله مى هم اله مم
محلا عر مدسا لم اى لا ما لاى كمر ماكم
مكى بهكم وبلا لما لمى لها مكر كم
الى ماكا بكسهم وبلامده ى هر لهم
حكى مر ما هراه اكرى ى هل
همم

115 Genghis Khan and his court. The Khan is seated on a throne decorated with Chinese dragons, with his wife at his side. On their knees in front of the throne are his two sons

116 The letter from Kayuk Khan to Pope Innocent IV, with its stamped signature, two centuries before the invention of printing in Europe

most effective means for the diffusion of culture and technology. It was in those years that some of the great Chinese inventions came to Europe. Gunpowder was first mentioned in Europe by Roger Bacon, the friend of that Guillaume de Rubrouck who had visited Karakorum. It was first used in the West, by both Christians and

Moslems, in the early fourteenth century. Printing also reached Europe from China during the period of the Mongol peace. The first printed document in Europe is perhaps the stamped signature of the reply of Kayuk Khan to the pope, written in Uighur script, which Giovanni da Piano Carpini brought from Karakorum and which, long unknown, was discovered in the Vatican archives in 1920.

Such was the beneficent *Pax Mongolica* which coincided with the European prosperity of the thirteenth century, and brought Christendom, as never before, into touch with the great, old civilizations of the East. But in the middle of the fourteenth century, this Mongol peace came to an end in anarchy and civil war. In the Far East, a national revolt in China ultimately brought the native Ming dynasty to power, and Karakorum itself was burnt. In the Middle East, Mongol rule collapsed in Persia; the great irrigation system of Mesopotamia, preserved for centuries, fell into ruin, and the anarchy was exploited by a new, temporary, destructive conqueror, Timur or Tamerlane. In the West, a new Turkish tribe, the Ottomans, displaced by the Mongol conquests, pushed into Europe, made their capital at Adrianople, and reduced the Greek emperor to vassalage. Thus the collapse of the Mongol Empire shook the fabric of society alike in China, in Islam, and in Europe. It was out of the anarchy in China, before the triumph of the Ming, that the Black Death came to Europe; it was during the anarchy of Islam that Ibn Khaldoun, in North Africa, elaborated his defeatist philosophy of history; and the convulsion of the Middle East, together with the collapse of the Mongol peace, dislocated the delicate mechanism of Europe's trade with the East. Indeed, the great caravan-route across Central Asia was finally broken: two centuries later, even its existence had been forgotten.

If the century from 1150 to 1250 can be seen as the highest point of medieval Europe, the century from 1350 to 1450 was, I suppose, the lowest. The old institutions had stiffened and a devitalized society could create no new, elastic institutions to replace them. In that period of contraction and reaction, of deadening clericalism and vain social revolt, intellectual life sank into formalism or took refuge

117 Timur, self-styled
restorer of the Mongol
Empire, advances on
Baghdad in 1401

from reality in satire, mysticism or myth. We have the good-
humoured satire of Boccaccio and Chaucer, the bitter satire of *Piers
Plowman*. We have the great medieval mystics, Suso and Tauler,
Richard Rolle and Thomas à Kempis. Above all, we have the archaic
myth of chivalry. Never was the spirit of feudalism so elaborate in
literature as when it was dead in fact: when feudal bonds were
rotted and feudal obligations ignored. It was while the princes of
Europe wasted their strength in treacherous usurpations and suicidal
civil wars that the sleek Flemish trencher-chaplain, Jean Froissart,
unctuously chronicled their glorious feats of arms, so unseasonably

interrupted by the 'shameful' protests and 'evil deeds' of those 'mischievous' or 'ungracious wretches', the hungry weavers and peasants, and it was when England was convulsed by royal usurpation and noble faction that that 'parfit gentle knight', Sir Thomas Malory, in prison (some would persuade us) for house-breaking, larceny, arson, rape and extortion, glorified, in his *Morte d'Arthur*, the archaic courtesies of the Round Table.

If a philosopher, trained in modern theories of cyclical history, were to place himself in the early fifteenth century, what, I wonder, would he conclude? At that time, it must have seemed that the future was not with Europe, frozen in archaic postures and privileges, not with Islam, helpless before successive invaders, but with China. China had provided almost all the technical innovations of Europe, and now, under its new Ming dynasty, it seemed set on a new policy of expansion. In the years 1405–33 the Chinese court-eunuch Chêng-Ho—one of the really great eunuchs of history (Justinian's general Narses is the other)—led or sent a series of naval expeditions which brought the whole Indian Ocean under Chinese control. Thanks to his enterprise, the rulers of India and Ceylon, the commercial centres of Malacca and Calicut paid their tribute or sent their exotic wares to China. Chinese fleets visited the Red Sea and the coast of East Africa. Only a little continuity was necessary and perhaps Chinese fleets, half a century later, would have arrived in Lisbon and London. Who would have supposed, at that time, that the reverse would happen: that instead, Portuguese fleets would arrive in Malacca and Calicut to divert the tribute of India and Ceylon westwards to Lisbon and Antwerp, and thereby initiate the new, half-millennial supremacy of Europe?

For this indeed is one of the apparent miracles of history. To explain it, Portuguese historians have discovered an almost fabulous character, Prince Henry of Portugal, 'the Navigator', the Chêng-Ho of the West (except that Prince Henry himself never went to sea), the solitary pioneer of European expansion, the founder of that trans-oceanic Portuguese Empire which was the first, and threatens to be the last, of European empires overseas. For some forty years, from about 1420 till his death in 1460, Prince Henry, we are told,

118 Prince Henry 'the Navigator' of Portugal. (Contemporary portrait by Nuno Gonçalves)

sat at Sagres, on the Atlantic tip of southern Portugal, surrounded by his cartographers and scientists, devising ever new and longer journeys. What inspired him? A crusading zeal against the Moslems of Africa? A dream of India? An image of the legendary Christian king in the East, Prester John? We do not know. We only know that in those years fleet after fleet sailed out from Portugal into the Atlantic, down the coast of Africa, preparing the way for the great sudden voyages, at the end of the century, of Bartholomew Dias and Vasco da Gama, and for the new empire of Asia and Brazil.

The legend of Prince Henry reads well; but let us not be bowled over by it. True history is not made by single heroes. At most, such figures are catalysts, or leaders of forces already there, and the question we must ask is not who inspired those new Portuguese voyages, or with what motive, but why, in the fifteenth century, when the rest of Europe was apparently fixed in social sclerosis and economic decline, one corner of it was able to break the spell and set this new example. For it was an example of great importance. Thanks to the free competition between the monarchies of Europe, all the other maritime powers of Europe would soon turn aside to follow it; that imitation, and that competition, would give to Europe its long ascendancy over the rest of the world.

What was the particular character of Portuguese society in the fifteenth century? This is a large, factual question, to which nevertheless I shall offer a short general answer: an answer drawn not only from these particular circumstances but also from other comparable turning-points in history, when the centre of power has moved from one part to another of a continent, or of the world.

For if history is to be seen, as I believe it should be seen, as a continuous process, then certain general conclusions always emerge. We find, for instance, that just as old institutions, unless they are continually adapted, will not serve new purposes, so new problems are rarely solved, in the first instance, by old societies. The reason can easily be guessed. Any society, so long as it is, or feels itself to be, a working society, tends to invest in itself: a military society tends to become more military, a bureaucratic society more bureaucratic, a commercial society more commercial, as the status and profits of war or office or commerce are enhanced by success, and institutions are framed to forward it. Therefore, when such a society is hit by a general crisis, it finds itself partly paralysed by the structural weight of increased social investment. The dominant military or official or commercial classes cannot easily change their orientation; and their social dominance, and the institutions through which it is exercised, prevent other classes from securing power or changing policy. If policy is to be changed to meet new circumstances we are more likely to find such a change, in the first instance, either in a complex elastic society—what today we would call a liberal society—in which different interests have separate, competing institutions, or in a less mature society: a society whose institutions have not been hardened and whose vested interests have not been deepened by past commitment. This general social truth, it seems to me, explains why it was not Ming China but fifteenth-century Europe, for all its temporary decline, which captured the next stage of history, and why, within fifteenth-century Europe, it was not Italy or Flanders or even France or England which showed the way, but a minuscule kingdom at the back end of eastward-looking Europe, Portugal.

We have seen, in the century from 1350, all Europe in crisis and the mature societies of Europe unable to create new institutions whereby to surmount that crisis. To say that they did nothing in that century would be an exaggeration. In numerous ways they responded to the challenge. Some new techniques were devised, some new forms of social organization were evolved. There was agricultural improvement: the landlord reaction had its brighter side. There was a revolution in cloth manufacture and in mining which made the fortune of new merchant cities in Germany. There was a development of gilds which, for a time, preserved a social balance in older cities. Princes, by extending their jurisdiction and absorbing new areas, sometimes increased their free-trade area and learned mercantile policies from the cities which they subjected. But, in general, what we see is over-emphasis on old forms; modification of old forms, perhaps, but not discovery of new. Landlords seek to preserve their power by reaction, not innovation. Capitalists, frustrated in trade, turn to banking or to land, or invest in taxes and offices. Even the gilds soon become restrictive and crush production in the cities in which they triumph: the economic decline of many a Swiss or German city was caused by this 'socialism' of the fifteenth century. In general, we may say that the existing structure of Europe, the structure acquired in the years of expansion, and strengthened by the passage of time and growth of interests, continues to absorb its energies, and by absorbing them, to use them up.

119 Craft-gilds: an apprentice mason and carpenter being examined by the Gild Warden before admission as master craftsmen

120 Ming dynasty ivory figure of a Chinese bureaucrat

Even the artistic Renaissance of the fifteenth century is not necessarily a sign of progress. Lavish patronage of the arts is perfectly compatible—as in the Baroque age—with economic decline. The new princes and their courtiers are often merchants who have switched their investment from trade to politics. Instead of increasing wealth by industry or commerce, they are accumulating it by taxation and dissipating it, through lack of other outlet, in conspicuous waste.

In Ming China it is the same. For centuries the Chinese Empire had lived on its bureaucracy of scholar-gentry, with which no dynasty could dispense. Foreign rulers might conquer central power, but always, in the end, they had turned to the Chinese bureaucracy in order to rule. Even the Mongols, in the end, had succumbed to it. They might prefer Uighurs or Christians at court; but there were not enough of them to go round the empire. So Kublai Khan ended by restoring the old bureaucracy, recruited by examination. When the nationalist Ming replaced the Mongols, they naturally returned with enthusiasm to the national system. Outwardly it might appear that Chêng-Ho was dished by a court intrigue; fundamentally, Chinese society was absorbed by its ancient structure, its ancient institutions.

But if China was a uniform, centralized empire, Europe's good fortune had always lain in its variety. If all Europe, like all China, had been centrally ruled, how different our history would have been! But in fact it was not so. In fact, in 1400, while the economic life of older Europe was being brought under princely control, there were some countries in which feudal institutions had taken but slender root, and one of those countries, happily placed for the new age, was Portugal.

The kingdom of Portugal, we have seen, had only been founded during the Second Crusade. It was a creation of northern Europe, like the kingdom of Jerusalem; and its very narrowness—a mere strip along the Atlantic coast—had protected it from the general fate of

121 Lisbon in the sixteenth century: a contemporary engraving

other societies in the fourteenth century. If Portugal, like Andalusia, had been reconquered from Islam by Castile, and governed from Burgos or Toledo, much of its economic life would no doubt have been drained away into the Spanish monarchy—as indeed was to happen after it was united with Spain in 1580. But because of its independence, and its smallness, it was forced to live by its own economy; and that economy lay on the sea. Portugal in the fifteenth century was like Genoa or Venice in the twelfth century, or Holland in the seventeenth: a small state forced by geography to look outwards to the sea. In the narrow space allowed to it there was no Portuguese feudalism powerful enough to absorb the mercantile life of its Atlantic coast; and in the great depression of the fourteenth century, when the mercantile cities of the Mediterranean turned away from commerce to land or banking—when Venice became a land-power and Genoa a finance-capital, and when Barcelona was swallowed up by the kingdom of Aragon—Lisbon retained its old character. It was still a capital of merchants and seamen, carrying salt to northern Europe, entering the internal markets of northern Europe, fishing and whaling in the Atlantic Ocean. It was now also a main port on the route from north to south Europe—the sea-route which was becoming more popular as the land-route suffered from the crisis of the times and the exactions of its rulers.

To Lisbon therefore, the new Venice, the new Genoa of the Atlantic, the heirs of the old Venice, the old Genoa of the Mediterranean would now turn. In the middle of the fourteenth century Italian merchants, squeezed out of Italy—the Bardi of Florence, the Lomellini of Genoa—converged on Lisbon, just as the *émigré* capitalists of Counter-Reformation Europe would converge on seventeenth-century Amsterdam. In 1391, when the Jews were slaughtered throughout Spain, the Jewish cartographers of Majorca —the best in Europe, the makers of the great medieval 'portulans' or sea-maps—fled to Portugal. The mercantile and scientific expertise of Italy, Flanders and of Catalonia was united, in Portugal, with the native shipbuilding industry; and the result was to make Portugal an economic and maritime force, as Venice and Genoa had been, as Amsterdam would be.

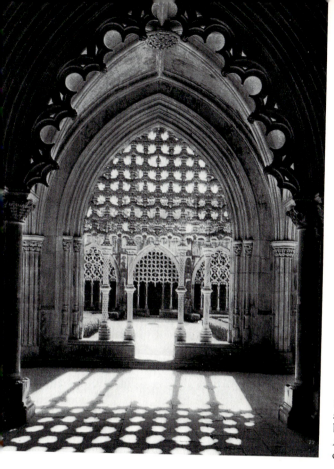

122 The Royal Cloister at the abbey of Batalha, built to celebrate the Anglo-Portuguese victory of Aljubarrota in 1385

As such, Portugal was brought into the wars of Europe. In the Hundred Years' War, that struggle of feudal princes for land in France, it was enlisted as the essential sea ally of England. It was to celebrate the Anglo-Portuguese victory of Aljubarrota that the great abbey of Batalha, the Battle Abbey of Portugal, was built. But the effect of the war, and the victory, was far more decisive for Portugal than for England. For Portugal, those years of war, 1383–5, were also years of internal revolution, a revolution which in form was dynastic, but which in substance went far deeper. It was a political and economic revolution which was the reverse of the other revolutions in Europe at that time. For whereas in the rest of Europe, in 189 those years of crisis, feudal or bureaucratic princes were absorbing the once free cities—the Medici would become despots of Florence and the Visconti of Milan and the Dukes of Burgundy would absorb the cities of Flanders—the city of Lisbon was, in effect, to absorb the new Anglo-Portuguese dynasty of Aviz. In Portugal, and only in Portugal, the 'feudal' nobility, with their 'feudal' fighting tastes, would accept, through the house of Aviz, the leadership of those maritime, mercantile forces which in the Mediterranean would be turning, under the seduction of a hardening social structure, from the sea to the land, from commerce to finance. The arts in Italy and Flanders would be bent to glorify the new princely state, and the myths of the Church which sustained it; but in Portugal even solid stone would soon be made to re-create, with its fantastic imagery of twisted cables and symbolic anchors, coral and shells and waves, the spirit of maritime journeys, commerce, and the distant seas.

The result was spectacular. With new leadership, new financial resources, new technical developments, the Portuguese mercantile state would send ever stouter ships out into the Atlantic in search of that African gold which, for so long, had been the motor of European commerce with the East. With the new growth of population in the fifteenth century, a new movement of expansion would be launched, comparable with that movement of which the Crusades had been a part; and this time it would be launched from Portugal. The pioneers were not necessarily Portuguese. Prince Henry's explorers who first reached the equator, Alvise de Cadamosto and Antoniotto Usodimare were, respectively, a Venetian and a Genoese. The techniques of colonization were not necessarily Portuguese: the wine- and the sugar-industries which the Portuguese and Spaniards would plant in the islands of the Atlantic were those which the Venetians and Genoese had first established in the islands of the Mediterranean. Chios and Crete were the models for Madeira and the Canaries: the wine of Madeira is Malmsey from Greece. But Portugal accepted the legacy of Italy, and passed it on. Columbus was a Genoese in the service of Spain; Magellan, a Portuguese, was also in the service of Spain; but the voyages of both, no less than

123 The instruments of expansion. A Catalan atlas commissioned by Char[

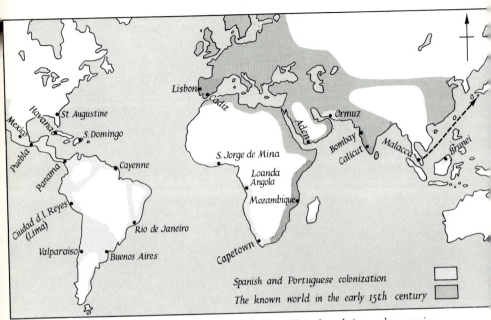

124 Portuguese and Spanish colonization in the late fifteenth and sixteenth centuries

those of Bartholomew Dias and Vasco da Gama, were technically prepared by Portugal. From that little corner of Europe, from that solitary revolution of 1383, in the period of European recession, Europe found the way to America, to India, and round the world.

With the discovery of those new worlds, the medieval history of Europe can be said to have come to an end. Thanks to those discoveries, and to the institutions which could exploit them (for once again, let me repeat, contact alone is nothing: it is the power to grasp and learn from contact which counts), as well as to the continued fragmentation and competition of the European states, Europe since 1500 has in fact dominated and transformed the world. Slowly, with difficulty, other powers followed the Portuguese lead. The 'feudal' monarchies of the West adapted themselves to the new opportunities; the 'feudal' chivalry which had wasted itself in European anarchy was turned once again, as in the eleventh century, outward; and a new age began.

In the map: Lisbon, Cadiz, Aden, Ormuz, Bombay, Calicut, Malacca, Brunei, Havana, St Augustine, S. Domingo, Mexico, Puebla, Panama, Cayenne, S. Jorge de Mina, Loanda Angola, Mozambique, Ciudad d.l. Reyes (Lima), Valparaiso, Rio de Janeiro, Buenos Aires, Capetown

Spanish and Portuguese colonization
The known world in the early 15th century

History never ends. There are great discoveries and great discontinuities, but neither are total in their effect. Great discoveries are merely local until a way of diffusion is found. Printing took 500 years to reach Europe from China. The fall of the Roman Empire in the West seems a great discontinuity, but we have seen that in many ways it was not: it was merely the abolition of a 'useless and expensive office' by a society which no longer needed it. The Arab conquest of the Middle East is certainly a great discontinuity. Syria and Egypt, till then, had been centres of Greek civilization; from then on they were 'Arabic'; and today they are the centres of Arabic civilization still. Even Persia, under that impact, became arabized—the greatest of historic empires abandoned its millennial religion and adopted the new, Arabic script. And yet even this great discontinuity was only partial. Greek science survived. Old pre-Arabic cults reasserted themselves within the framework of Islam, or co-existed with it—for it was not till the fourteenth century, that century of general contraction, that Islam, like Christianity, became intolerant of its minorities. After the violent momentary disturbance, the balance settled again around its old centre: historic Persia absorbed the Arab caliphate just as historic China would absorb the Mongols. Whenever we look at the great apparent breaches or turning-points of history, we see, beneath the spectacular cracks in the surface, the slow, cohesive continuum underneath. This does not mean that the breaches have not occurred. Of course they have, and it would be absurd to ignore them. It only means that they are not complete. There is no such thing, in history, as a clean break.

Nevertheless, historians have to make clean breaks. I have made mine in the middle of the fifteenth century. Naturally, it is an artificial break, and already I hear querulous voices protesting, both at what I have put in and at what I have left out. Why have I stopped with the Portuguese voyages, I shall be asked, as if they alone pointed the way to the future? What of the Italian *Quattrocento*? If Prince Henry looks forward, does Cosimo de' Medici look back? Is not the 'Renaissance', the 'Revival of Letters', as important a springboard of modern Europe as the voyages of Vasco da Gama and Columbus; the rediscovery of Greece as the 'discovery' of Asia and America?

Of course, of course . . . and yet still I find myself doubting. Every change in history, every shift in the centre of gravity of civilization, is a complex process, and its inspiration often comes from the old mature society that is being replaced. But that does not mean that the old society creates the new. Hellenistic Greece did not create Rome, nor Byzantium Italy. The societies which look forward are not those which transmit ideas, nor even, necessarily, those which generate them: they are those which can seize them and exploit them. Renaissance Italy transmitted the ideas of Antiquity to all Europe. It generated some of the ideas of modernity. But where were those ideas applied? The ideas of Machiavelli, Bruno, Galileo were driven out of Italy. Italian society did not want them. They were welcomed, disseminated and applied in other societies.

As for art—the art of the Renaissance, art in general—where does it stand in the process of history? It is tempting to see an artistic efflorescence as a sign of social dynamism, but is the equation true? 'Art happens', said Whistler, and sometimes this seems the best and only possible observation on the subject. How many great poets have lived and died 'leaving great verses to a little clan'? At other times we see art created, or at least sustained, by the mechanics of patronage; and patronage reflects many social forms, not all of them progressive. There is the patronage of communes, of mercantile aristocracies, of princes, of popes. Sometimes patronage is best maintained by a static, unequal society with a privileged, unproductive, tax-consuming aristocracy. To an economist, the Italian Renaissance does not represent vitality but the investment in conspicuous waste of swollen taxes which, in a stagnant economy, can find no more productive use. Artistic genius, like all genius, is unpredictable; but how much a society invests in art depends less on the vitality of that society than on its form. The 'bastard feudalism' of the late Middle Ages produced works of elaborate beauty; so did the princely courts, and especially the papal court, of seventeenth-century Italy. But who would draw the consequence that these were the social forms of human progress?

So half-reluctantly (for who does not prefer the house of Medici to the house of Aviz?), I cling to my position and, since I must make a break, I date the beginning of Europe's mastery not from the 'Revival of Letters', that last brilliant efflorescence of medieval Italy, but from the great maritime voyages of the Atlantic societies which, for their new purposes, drew on the expertise of that older world. From that moment, as it seems to me, for all the substantial continuity of history, a new age can be dated, and therefore my present subject can be closed. For in these pages I have chosen only to deal with the centuries before the great European 'take-off': the centuries which, increasingly, are neglected in the teaching of modern history: what I have called the centuries of recovery.

How remote they seem! And yet, are they really so remote? Our ancestors in the eighteenth century chose to dismiss them as centuries of Gothic barbarism. Our ancestors of the nineteenth century, rejecting that enlightened disdain, saw them through a romantic haze, and made them seem more distant still. Some modern historians write as if the whole Middle Ages consisted in the administration of archdeaconries. But I believe that those ages are far nearer to us than is often supposed. Historical parallels can never be drawn without risk, but general lessons can be extracted even from societies distant in time as in place. In this survey I have suggested certain general lessons, which may be applicable to other societies in other times. Some may even be applicable to our own time.

For instance, I have suggested that if recovery is never automatic, at least decline need not be final. The line of progress may not be straight, or even continuous, for history presents many obstacles: social petrifaction here, political decay there, demographic failure, disease, mere accident, and the register of human crime and folly. Through these obstacles history is the story of social forces, of the rejuvenation or sclerosis of institutions, of the fertile or infertile contact of ideas. We can see our own place in the process today. Today, after a long period of predominance, we have gone through a structural crisis which may be compared with that of the fourteenth century. We have had our loss of colonies, our Mongol Empire, our social troubles, our Hundred Years' War. But I do not think that we should therefore suppose that European history is closed. The history of the past may help to explain what one of the most distinguished living historians—I refer to the great Dutch historian Pieter Geyl—has called 'the vitality of western civilization'.

LIST OF DATES

1366	Ottoman Turks establish their capital in Europe, at Adrianople	1405	Chinese conquest of Ceylon begins Chinese maritime expansion to the West
1368–1644	Ming dynasty		
1378–1417	'Great Schism' of Roman Church	1415	John Huss burnt
		1419–36	Hussite wars in Bohemia
1379–82	Industrial revolts in Flanders (Philip van Artevelde) and Italy (i Ciompi)	1420	Portuguese occupation of Madeira: beginning of Portuguese overseas expansion
1380–1405	Career of Timur (Tamerlane)	1444	Battle of Varna: beginning of Turkish expansion in Europe
1381	Peasants' Revolt in England		
		1453	Turks capture Constantinople
1382	Wyclif's doctrines condemned	1479	Turks conquer Albania
1383–5	Revolution in Portugal: battle of Aljubarrota (1385) and establishment of Aviz dynasty	1487–92	Completion of Christian Reconquest in Spain
		1492	Columbus discovers America
1391	General massacre of the Jews in Spain	1498	Vasco da Gama discovers searoute to India

BIBLIOGRAPHICAL NOTES

THE STAGES OF PROGRESS

The great works of eighteenth-century 'sociological' history to which I refer are, above all, Voltaire's *Essai sur les Mœurs* (1754–69), Hume's *History of England* (1754–61), William Robertson's *History of Charles V* (1769) and *History of America* (1788), and, of course, greatest of all, Gibbon's *Decline and Fall of the Roman Empire* (1776–87). All were influenced, especially, by Montesquieu's *De l'Esprit des Lois* (1748). Ibn Khaldoun's famous work of historical philosophy, the *Muqaddimah*, was written in 1377: I have written a short essay on him, and it, in my *Historical Essays* (London 1957). An English translation of the *Muqaddimah* by F. Rosenthal has since been published (New York 1958).

The obsession with decay and death in the fifteenth century is apparent in any study of its art. I think particularly of Alberto Tenenti, *La Vie et la Mort à travers l'Art du XVe siècle* (Paris 1952), and the magnificent work of Emile Mâle, from whose *L'Art Religieux . . . après le Concile de Trent* (Paris 1951) I take the quotation about Michelangelo. The remarks of Busbequius on the Turkish menace come from his four long Latin letters from Constantinople.

The achievements of the Byzantines, at least in scientific theory, in the sixth century AD, are described by S. Sambursky in his book *The Physical World of Later Antiquity* (London 1962). The debt of Europe to China is shown in Joseph Needham, *Science and Civilisation in China* (Cambridge 1954–).

The concept of 'the Renaissance' has recently attracted much scholarly attention. For an account of Michelet's invention of the term see Lucien Fèbvre's essay, 'Comment Jules Michelet inventa la Renaissance' in his *Pour une Histoire à part Entière* (Paris 1962). The tendency of modern scholars is to dilute the fifteenth-century Renaissance, sharing out among other periods the achievements which their predecessors had concentrated in the fifteenth and early sixteenth centuries.

My interpretation of the decline of Rome is based largely on the works of Ferdinand Lot (*La Fin du Monde Antique et le Debut du Moyen Age*, Paris 1951), Michael Rostovtzeff (*Social and Economic History of the Roman Empire*, 2nd edn., 2 vols., Oxford 1957), and Ernst Stein (*Histoire du Bas Empire*, 2 vols., Brussels 1949, 1959). Rostovtzeff's theory that the army of the later empire was the instrument of peasant victory over the towns has been challenged and shown to be overdrawn (see Norman Baynes, *Byzantine Studies and Other Essays*, London 1955, pp. 307f.); but the ruralization of the empire in the third century seems undeniable. For the cities of the empire see A. H. M. Jones, *The Greek City* (Oxford 1940). On the mystery-religions I have used mainly the excellent work of Franz Cumont, *Les Religions Orientales dans le Paganisme Romain* (Paris 1909; English translation, Chicago 1911) and for Persia R. C. Zaehner, *The Dawn and Twilight of Zoroastrianism* (London 1961) and F. C. Burkitt, *The Religion of the Manichees* (Cambridge 1925). Christianity in Egypt and North Africa is illustrated by W. H. Frend, *The Donatist Church* (Oxford 1952) and 'The Failure of the Persecutions in the Roman Empire' in *Past and Present*, No. 16 (1959). That heresy was national as well as social has been doubted by A. H. M. Jones (in *Journal of Theological Studies*, 1959); but I venture to think that he sees nationalism in too narrowly political a light: I believe that heresy consecrates the sense of national distinctness, regardless of political aspirations, and I find it difficult, on any other hypothesis, to explain so general a phenomenon. For the barbarian invasions Thomas Hodgkin, *Italy and Her Invaders* (4 vols., Oxford 1892) remains a magnificent narrative source.

THE DARK AGES

Henri Pirenne, *Mahomet et Charlemagne* (English translation, London 1939) raised a great deal of controversy which has now been conveniently collected in *The Pirenne Controversy*, a volume in the series *Problems in European History*, ed. Alfred F. Havinghurst (Boston 1958). For the nomad invasions I have used especially E. A. Thompson, *A History of Attila and The Huns* (Oxford 1948) and E.-F. Gautier, *Genseric Roi des Vandales* (Paris 1951). My knowledge of the camel-nomads comes from E.-F. Gautier, *Le Passé de l'Afrique du Nord: Les Siècles Obscurs* (Paris 1942) and of Persia from Arthur Christensen, *L'Iran sous les Sassanides* (2nd edn., Copenhagen 1944). A vivid picture of monasticism in the Dark

Ages is given in Christopher Dawson, *Religion and The Rise of Western Culture* (London 1950). The position of the Vikings in the economy of the Dark Ages is shown by A. R. Lewis, *The Northern Seas* (Princeton 1958) and Sture Bolin, 'Mohammed, Charlemagne and Ruric' in *Scandinavian Historical Review*, I (1953). The great work on the early slave-trade is C. Verlinden, *L'Esclavage dans l'Europe Médiévale* (vol. I, Bruges 1955); see also Marc Bloch, 'Le Problème de l'Or au Moyen Age' (*Annales d'Hist. Econ. et Soc.*, v) and Maurice Lombard, 'L'Or Musulman du VIIe au XIe Siècle' in *Annales, Economies, Sociétés, Civilisations*, 1947. Finally, for the history of the stirrup, see Lynn White, jnr., *Medieval Technology and Social Change* (Oxford 1961), and for some illuminating general observations on the whole subject of the nomadic invaders and the Persian great horses see William McNeill, *The Rise of the West* (Chicago 1963).

THE CRUSADES

There are many histories of the Crusades, from Thomas Fuller's *The Holy War* (1639) onwards: in English the obvious modern account is Sir Steven Runciman's *A History of the Crusades* (3 vols., Cambridge 1951–4). There is also an excellent brief account by Sir Ernest Barker (*The Crusades*, in The World's Manuals, 1925); Voltaire's account is in his *Essai sur les Mœurs*. For agricultural change I have again used Lynn White, *Medieval Technology and Social Change*; but this writer's treatment of the plough has been strongly criticized (see R. H. Hilton's review in *Past and Present*, No. 24, April 1963). The standard work on the plough is ffrancis Payne, 'The Plough in Ancient Britain' in *Archaeological Journal*, CIV (1947). The background of the Christian Re-conquest in Spain, with the influence of Cluny and the cult of Santiago, is illustrated in Américo Castro, *The Structure of Spanish History* (trans. Edmund L. King, Princeton 1954), and in Gerald Brenan's wonderful work *The Literature of the Spanish People* (Cambridge 1951). For the advance in east Germany see F. L. Carsten, *The Origins of Prussia* (Oxford 1954). For the revival of towns, I have relied largely on Henri Pirenne, *Medieval Cities, Their Origins and the Revival of Trade* (trans. Frank D. Halsey, Princeton 1948), Yves Renouard, *Les Hommes d'Affaires Italiens du Moyen Age* (Paris 1949), J. Lestocquoy, *Les Villes de Flandre et d'Italie* (Paris 1952), and Fritz Rörig, *Die Europäische Stadt im Mittelalter* (Göttingen 1955); for the revival of gold coinage, on Marc Bloch, 'Le Problème de l'Or au Moyen Age' in *Annales d'Hist. Econ. et Soc.*, v, and *Esquisse d'Histoire Monétaire* (Paris 1949).

The great work on this subject is C. H. Haskins, *The Renaissance of the Twelfth Century* (Cambridge, Mass. 1927). For the struggles generated by the new learning see G. Paré, A. Brunet, P. Tremblay, *La Renaissance du XII*e *Siecle* (Paris and Ottawa 1933); for the founding of the universities, Hastings Rashdall, *Universities of Europe in the Middle Ages* (new edn., Oxford 1936); for heresy, H. C. Lea, *The History of the Inquisition in The Middle Ages*. A good general history is David Knowles, *The Evolution of Medieval Thought* (London 1962). William Stubbs, *Seventeen Lectures on the Study of Medieval and Modern History* (3rd edn., Oxford 1900) contains useful essays on the intellectual atmosphere of the court of Henry II. The quotation from Macaulay is from his essay on Ranke's *History of the Popes.*

EUROPE TURNS WEST

The failure of the Franks in Greece is illustrated in the great work of W. Miller, *The Latins in the Levant* (London 1908), and in Palestine, more briefly, in Sir Steven Runciman's essay *The Families of Outremer* (London 1960). The successive banking crises are described in Yves Renouard, *Les Hommes d'Affaires Italiens du Moyen Age* (Paris 1949). For the Black Death I have used L. F. Hirst, *The Conquest of Plague* (Oxford 1953), Charles Creighton, *A History of Epidemics in Britain* (Cambridge 1891) and for other details C. Verlinden, 'La Peste Noire en Espagne' in *Revue Belge de Philosophie et d'Histoire* (1938), and Robert Höniger, *Gang und Verbreitung des Schwarzen Todes in Deutschland . . .* (Berlin 1881). The 'landlord reaction' must similarly be traced in national histories. The investment of cities like Venice and Barcelona in land is illustrated, for instance, by Roberto Cessi, *Storia della Repubblica di Venezia* (Milan 1946) and J. Vicens Vives, *Historia Económica de España* (Barcelona 1959). The transformation of the monasteries into mere landlords, at least in England, is vividly illustrated in the works of David Knowles—perhaps most graphically in the anthology of personal portraits extracted from those works and published under the title *Saints and Scholars* (Cambridge 1962). The authority whom I have quoted on the absorption of tithes is G. C. Coulton, *Scottish Abbeys and Social Life* (Cambridge 1932). For the urban troubles in Flanders see especially Henri Pirenne, *Belgian Democracy and its Early History* (Manchester 1915). My quotation is from his *Economic and Social History of Medieval Europe* (London 1937). For the urban troubles in Italy I have used N. Rodolico, *I Ciompi* (Florence 1945). For Bohemia see Karl Kautzky, *Communism in Central Europe* (London 1897). For the Mongols see R. Grousset, *L'Empire des Steppes* (Paris 1939); and for the diffusion of techniques in the Mongol period, especially, T. F. Carter, *The Invention of Printing in China and its Spread Westward* (2nd edn., New York 1955).

The rise of Portugal as a sea-power can be followed in E. A. Prestage, *The Portuguese Pioneers* (London 1933); but for an explanation of the phenomenon I have found one book of the greatest interest, and so I mention it, though written in Portuguese. It is Vitorino Magelhães Godinho, *A Economia dos Descubrimentos Henriquinos* (Lisbon 1963).

LIST OF ILLUSTRATIONS

82 Fountains Abbey, Yorkshire; eleventh century and later. Photo: Aerofilms

83 Pisa port; late thirteenth-century relief. Museum of Ligurian Architecture and Sculpture, Genoa

84 The Treaty of Tunis, 1270. Archives Nationales, Paris, MS J 937, fol. 1

85 Castle of Geoffrey de Brières at Karytaina, Greece; thirteenth century. Painting by Edward Lear. Geunadeion Library, Athens. Photo: Lutz Braun

86 Templar seal; 1259. Archives Nationales, Paris.

87 Schoolroom scene in the twelfth century. From a psalter written and illustrated by Eadwine, a monk of Christ Church, Canterbury; c. 1150. Trinity College, Cambridge

88 St Hildebrand (Pope Gregory VII). From a painting by C. Savolini; seventeenth century. San Domenico, Cesena. Photo: A. Villani

89 The emperor Henry IV pleads with Mathilda of Tuscany and Abbot Hugo of Cluny. From the *Vita Mathildis*. Biblioteca Apostolica Vaticana, Rome, MS Lat. 4922, fol. 49 recto

90 Abelard and Héloise. Carved capital in the Salle des Gardes of the Conciergerie, Paris; fourteenth century. Photo: Archives Photographiques

91 Aristotle and Alexander. From the *Khamsa* of Nizami; c. 1500. British Museum, MS 246, fol. 227 (Royal Asiatic Society's Collection)

92 Socrates and Alexander. From the *Khamsa* of Nizami; c. 1500. British Museum, MS 246, fol. 311 (Royal Asiatic Society's Collection)

93 Page from Arabic translation of the first part of Galen's treatise on electuaries; ascribed to Johannes Grammaticus. Nationalbibliothek, Vienna, Cod. AF 10, fol. 15

94 The universe according to Ptolemy. Diagram from Oronce Finé, *Théorique de la huictième sphère et sept planètes*; 1528

95 The emperor Frederick II of Sicily with one of his sons. Relief by Maestro Nicola; 1229. Bitonto Cathedral, Apulia. Photo: Lala Aufsberg

96 Castel del Monte, Apulia; c. 1240. Photo: Lala Aufsberg

97 Carved ivory box from Cordoba; 967. Louvre, Paris. Photo: Giraudon

98 Reliefs of falconry, by Niccolo or Giovanni Pisano; late thirteenth century. Fontana Maggiore, Perugia. Photo: Mansell/Alinari

99 Donation of a schoolhouse by St Louis, king of France, in 1256. Archives Nationales, Paris, MS S 6219, fol. 85

100 Plato. From a stained glass window in the church of St Dionys, Esslingen, Germany; c. 1300. Photo: Landesbildstelle Württemberg

101 Aristotle. From a stained glass window in the church of St Dionys, Esslingen, Germany; c. 1300. Photo: Landesbildstelle Württemberg

102 Albi Cathedral; founded in 1277. Photo: Martin Hürlimann

103 St Dominic and St Francis. Terracotta by Andrea della Robbia; late fifteenth century. Loggia di San Paolo, Florence. Photo: Mansell/Brogi

104 The battle of Crécy. From the *Chroniques de Froissart*. Bibliothèque Nationale, Paris. Photo: Giraudon

105 The Black Death: burning of infected clothes. Bodleian Library, Oxford, MS 264, fol. 83 recto

106 Burial scene at Tournai, 1349, from the *Annales* of Gilles de Muisit. Bibliothèque Royale, Brussels, MS 13076, fol. 24 verso. Photo: Giraudon

107 German 'plague cross'; fourteenth century. Stadtmuseum, Cologne. Photo: Rheinisches Bildarchiv

108 Chaucer's Monk, from the Ellesmere Chaucer. Huntington Library, California, MS HM EL 26 C9

209

INDEX